Life in the 'Boat

These stories originally appeared in the *Steamboat Pilot & Today.*
They are reprinted with permission.

Printed in the United States of America.

Cover design by Sue Schneller;
www.kidsillustrations.com.

Booklocker.com, Inc.
www.booklocker.com
2008

Life in the 'Boat

How I fell on Warren Miller's skis, cheated on my hairdresser and fought off the Fat Fairy...true tales from Ski Town U.S.A.

Joanne Palmer

Dedication

For Peter
Love you 10 times a million
and then some.

Acknowledgements

It takes a village to raise a child, but to write a book, raise a child and run your own business takes something bigger. It takes a galaxy of amazing people. For the past two years, I've been blessed with a core group of people who have offered cheerleading, support, insta-edits, brainstorming and lots of hand-holding. Thank you all so much.

The shining stars in my galaxy:

Laura Palmer, heartfelt thanks for talking me off the ledge of self-doubt a thousand times and helping me rewrite and revise. I'd be lost without you.

Helen Palmer, the original funny woman and great storyteller.

Mark Palmer, who keeps me smiling.

The mud season writer's group: Elizabeth Bartasius. LA Bourgeois, Susana Field, Debbi Funston, Lu Etta Loeber and Jill Murphy Long

Lori Bourgeois, I hit the friend jackpot when I met you. I can never thank you enough for your ideas, edits, yummy recipes and great wine!

Bettina Martens, uber friend.

Meg Montgomery and Angela Robinson, thank you for never saying 'no'.

Mrs. Muse a.k.a. Barbara Jones, for brainstorming and making me laugh.

Ken Neis, the love of my life. Thank you for helping me find the humor in all things and not complaining when the alarm went off at 6 a.m.

Margaret Doner, for her lifelong friendship and faith in me.

Peter Bollenbacher, thank you for providing so much inspiration and joy.

Table of Contents

Introduction 1

Chapter One: Life At Home 3
    I Cheated On My Hairdresser 5
    When Mother Nature Writes 7
    Gentlemen, Start Your Engines 9
    Traffic Is Killing My Pie Obsession 11
    Having A Towanda Moment 13
    Snoops Need More Scoop 15
    Hunting for Groceries 17
    Warning Signs of Cabin Fever 19
    Steamboat Resume 22
    Construction Town U.S.A. 25

Chapter Two: Life At Home 27
    Clowning Around 29
    A Dog's Life Is Good Enough For Me 31
    The Seven Stages of Garage Sales 33
    Do Not Send Me a Postcard 35
    Celery Gimmicks 37
    Grouch Potato 39
    Six Words Or Less 41
    Clock Changing and Quantum Physics 43
    Together We Have It All 45
    The Beer Is Behind the Jelly, Dear 47
    My Knight in Shining Dungarees 49
    Our Lady of the Perpetual Washing Machine 51
    I Owe It All to Thin Mints 53
    Real Estate Mogul, Not 55

Chapter Three: Life On The Road 57
    Countdown to Departure 59
    Travel Policies 61

Happy Camper? 63
Hair Mousse and Toe Cleavage 65

Chapter Four: Life During The Holidays 67
Busted! 69
Did I Mention the Tiara? 71
Labor Pains 73
Happy New-Thanks-Mas-Ween 75
The First Fight of the Holidays Is With the Tree 77
Reduce, Reuse, Recycle, Regift? 79
Holiday Horoscopes 81
A Local Dedication 83
A Lifetime of Guilt 86

Chapter Five: Life with My Body 89
Memorandum 91
Dear Dictionary 93
The Fat Fairy Strikes Again 95
Rest for the Weary 97
Body by Bifocals 99

Chapter Six: Life as A Mother 101
Keeping Time with the Refrigerator 103
Dating and the Single Mom 105
Calling Detroit 107
So Not Cool 109
Go Ahead Take My Day 111
Who Wants To Be Frugal If You Have To Be A Tightwad? 113
Losing My Mind 115
Raising the Dead 117
Dude, That Was Awesome! 119
Confessions of a Lacrosse Mom 121
I Yike Hammers 123

Chapter Seven: Life during Ski Season **125**
I Say, "Right On!" 127
Who Said There Are No Stupid Questions? 129
The Four Stages of Winter 131
I've Got the Genes for Embarrassing Moments 133
Resist Temptation 135

Chapter Eight: Life with Technology **137**
In Love with Mr. Mail 139
Not Just For Talking 141
This Time I Mean It 143
Press 3 to Send Me to Fiji 145
For Emergencies — Or Everything 147

Introduction

In the beginning, there was guilt. Motherhood guilt. The worse kind of guilt there is. If you multiply Catholic guilt by not-going-to-the-gym guilt and quadruple the total and top it off with a dash of calorie guilt, you still will not fully comprehend the enormity of motherhood guilt.

No one is better than dishing out guilt than a mother and no one is better at feeling guilt than oh, say, a mother.

Mothers feel guilty for just about everything.

If they work, they feel guilty they are not at home with their children.

If they are at home, they feel guilty they are not at work.

If they feed Cocoa Krispies to their children for breakfast instead of wholesome granola they feel guilty.

As soon as my son was born, the guilt began. I felt guilty I didn't use cloth diapers and clogged the landfill with disposables. I felt guilty I didn't puree my own organic baby food. I felt guilty when I let him watch cartoons instead of reading a book to him on quantum physics. All of this guilt, however, was a blip, a trifle, a mere ping in comparison to the crushing guilt I bore for not doing his baby book.

I have no excuse. I got two at my baby shower but I never filled them out.

I'm SORRY.

Even though I typed, 'sorry' in capital letter the mantle of guilt continues to weigh heavily on my shoulders.

The day my son rolled over is not recorded in his baby book. The day he got up on all fours and crawled is not written in the baby book. And the day he blinked, burped and ballyhooed is not in his baby book. I had new mom friends that not only did baby books, they progressed to videos and scrapbooks, all duly noting every baby movement and milestone. I had new mom friends who crocheted baby blankets and knit darling, cozy, fleecy hoodies and booties.

I did nothing.

Nothing.

Once, I attended a photo scrap booking class full of good intentions of making a beautiful leather photo album he could one day show his grandchildren. I bought the starter kit, the special scissors and the album. But, then, I did nothing.

Nothing.

Nine years later, I spied a column in the *Steamboat Pilot & Today* asking for column ideas by then-editor Scott Stanford. Still plagued with guilt about the darn baby book and that all of Peter's photos and artwork were gathering dust in boxes, I called. I begged. I badgered. I babbled. Because Scott is from South Carolina, he has impeccable manners and just to placate me he very politely suggested I e-mail him some sample columns. I'm sure he hoped he'd never hear from me again. But, I sent him some samples and hounded him until he gave me space in the Sunday paper. When Scott became advertising director and Brent Boyer took his spot, Brent moved me into my current position on page two of Wednesday's paper.

On my two-year anniversary of writing, "Life in the 'Boat," I decided to self-publish these columns into a book Peter can later give to his therapist.

"This," he'll say, choking back tears, "chronicles my childhood. No videos. No photo albums. No baby book."

Until Peter grows up, or I run out of motherhood guilt (never!), I hope to keep writing this column. Heartfelt thanks to Scott and Brent for taking a chance on me. And thank-you, dear readers, for your support.

Chapter One: Life At Home

I Cheated On My Hairdresser

In a small town, secrets are hard to keep—especially beauty secrets. Which is why I was a fool to do the unthinkable.

I cheated on my hairdresser.

I swore I'd never do it. There was no third party. It was finances, not fickleness, that made me stray. My bank account was lean, my roots were long and I slipped. I decided to buy hair color in a box and do it myself. It seemed easy enough. But as I stood in the aisle looking at all the boxes, I was instantly confused. Of course there was ash blonde, strawberry blonde and champagne blonde. But Dulce de Leche Blonde? It sounded more like a Starbucks drink than hair color. I furtively selected golden blonde, and snuck out of the store.

That night, I pulled on plastic gloves and went to work. It was lonely. It was too quiet. I missed the buzz of blow dryers in the salon, the free cookies, the pitcher of water with lemons floating on top. There was no swirl of conversation as women waited for their color to brighten, their nails to dry, their heels to soften in the pedicure tubs.

"Did you see Suri Cruise on the cover of Vanity Fair?" I asked the dog. She cocked her head and scratched.

I shook the tube, squirted on the color, bundled my hair on top of my head, then called a friend,

"In 20 minutes I'll either be golden blonde or blind," I said.

"What?"

I explained that, according to the directions, if I got any of this smelly goopy golden blonde color in my eyes it might make me blind. My friend thought it served me right for committing hair adultery.

"What if you run into Sally at the grocery store?"

"I'll go to the other one."

Of course I knew where she shopped, and whether she was a post office or cluster box kind of gal. I knew the names of her kids, her dogs and her husband's birthday. What I couldn't remember is how we met. No matter, once we did, we stayed together for seven years. She changed hair salons twice, and I followed behind her like a puppy. She left for the Front Range for a year, but as soon as she returned, so did I.

She saw me through champagne highlights with red lowlights. She politely refused (thank heavens!) when I asked her to cut my hair like Winona Ryder's. She layered my hair after my divorce, and then patiently waited with

5

me until it grew out. When I begged, she changed me into a brunette and then never said, "I told you so" when she transformed me back into a blonde.

Only Sally knew I was a closet curler. My fine blonde hair needs more than product. I have to apply product, blow dry it upside down, apply more product, spend a few minutes rolling my limp locks around squishy curlers, blow dry it again, take the curlers out and then mist it and the bathroom with hairspray. An hour later, it's flat and goes into a ponytail.

Sally laughed at my hair follies as she willingly shared her parenting tips and her recipe for funeral potatoes. She never caused me to kick the sink and run out of the salon in tears as I did once in Washington, D.C. That hairdresser, who had a fake French accent and wore his shirt unbuttoned to his navel, cut a foot from my hair when I'd asked for a trim.

"Trust me bab-eee," he purred. "You'll love it when it's blown dried."

I did not.

Hairdressers know—even more than Santa Claus—when you've been bad or good. So I figured Sally probably already heard about my home hair coloring fiasco. But would she forgive me and take me back?

I'll have to call and find out.

When Mother Nature Writes

To: The Seasons

From: Mother Nature

Re: Performance

Date: May 21, 2008

It has come to my attention that the residents of Steamboat Springs are getting annoyed with me, Mother Nature. Therefore, the following memo will review the most recent performance of each season with a suggested plan for improved performance and productivity. Please implement all suggestions immediately. Let's get our ducks in a row!

SPRING-Your performance has been unsatisfactory. Punctuality is a big, big problem. The first day of spring was March 20th. Where have you been? Your excessive tardiness will no longer be tolerated. It appears to me you have been spending too much time with Old Man Winter. Please be advised that interoffice romance is discouraged.

Not only has your performance been unsatisfactory it has been erratic. One day it's warm (Mother's Day was appreciated) BUT then you follow it up with a week of snow, wind and rain. I am getting impatient; I'm ready for the flowers to bloom. It is time for the residents to put away their snow shovels and get out their gardening gear. They want to put their geraniums outside without fear of frost.

Suggested improvements: I am sending you to at a three-day Time Management seminar. Attendance is mandatory. Please don't be late.

SUMMER-A short but adequate performance last year. Consistency seems to be an issue with you. Last year there were no enough temperature fluctuations....you were red-hot all of the time. This is the high country, not the Sahara. Yes, yes I'm fully aware of global warming. In fact, former vice-president Gore gave me a private viewing of his slide show. Loved it! But I'm not ready to go there yet.

Suggested improvements: Please interface with spring to ensure a seamless and **gradual** transition. The residents do not like it when it's spring one day and summer the next. Ease them into it.

AUTUMN- Last year your performance was very good. But there appears to be scheduling conflicts. You extended your season into winter's by weeks giving the residents such a scare they delayed the opening of the ski area.

Suggested improvements: You need to interface with the Aspen department and put on a better show with the leaves this year.

WINTER-Excellent performance! However, overtime expenditures were outrageous! In case you have misplaced your manual, "Mother Nature's Mandates" which outlines all operating procedures, I would like to remind you that overtime expenditures must be approved in advance. Please prepare a projected overtime budget for the ski season 2008-9 and submit to accounting immediately. The Mother Nature call center logged hundreds of calls (quite a few from Jill Murphy Long) reminding me they love snow. They moved here knowing full well they'd measure snow in feet instead of inches and that entire days might be devoted to shoveling the stuff. However! One irate resident complained she lost her green beans to snow on the Fourth of July. July! Mother Nature checked the frost dates for fall and found that the first frost date was listed as August 16th. The last frost date of the previous season? August 17th. Winter is empire building and this activity can no longer be tolerated. These turf wars must stop!

Your relationship with the Department of Sun must improve. You two need to work together to provide sunny days and fresh snow.

Suggested improvements: I am sending you to a Team Building Seminar (yes, it's in Silverthorne so you can stop and shop at Target). Attendance is mandatory.

Thank you for your attention to these matters. Let's hit the ground running and make it a great year!

Gentlemen, Start Your Engines

Writer Henry James once said the most beautiful words in the English language were *summer afternoon. Summer afternoon.* Quite possibly these were the two most beautiful words until one other word crept into the English language: *lawnmower. Lawnmower.* Ugh. Just saying the word is a bad experience.

Lawnmowers are ugly, loud, gas-guzzling beasts with manly brand names: Toro, Yard Man, Snapper, Scots*man* and my personal favorite: Lawn-Boy. They have torque ratings, auto chokes, gobs of horsepower and even anti-vibration systems. There are lawn tractors, zero-turn-radius mowers, mulching mowers and self propelled mowers—all equally designed to ruin a summer siesta. Because you know and I know that just as you settle down for a snooze someone in the 'hood will crank up a lawnmower and do their best to blow you right out of the hammock.

Based on absolutely nothing but my own observations while walking the dog, here are the five lawn mower types I've identified so far this season. (Yes, I know there are women who mow but right now I feel like picking on men).

Type One: Bazooka Dude

This person has a teeny tiny patch of grass--usually about 10' x 10', yet he feels the need to attack it with the full force of a bazooka mower. And so he mounts up on lawn tractor to wage war against a few innocent blades of grass. I could rival Freud with the psychological significance of this guy, but instead, I'm going to sum up the situation with a catchy Texas saying: "Big hat, no cattle."

Type Two: Rocker Dude

This guy dons his Grateful Dead T-shirt, cranks up his iPod, guns the lawnmower and gets after it. Occasionally he breaks for a beer and to play air guitar but sure shootin' he's having a great time. He may be wearing a hearing aid next year but for now he's singing, "Uncle John's Band" and hoping to reclaim his youth. Let's just hope he doesn't try out for "American Idol."

Type Three: Nudie Dudie

Ah, the exertion of wheeling his lawnmower out of the garage inspires nudie dudie to shed his shirt. Don't rush to find your binoculars. Nudie dudie plans to take his time getting a full upper body workout in. Mow. Flex. Mow. Flex. By the time he's finished strutting his stuff he may have sunburn on those lily-white pecs.

Type Four: BMX Dude

He likes the natural look and so his lawn resembles a BMX course full of dirt, rocks, and obstacles. Nevertheless, the BMX dude knows he can triumph over with it with a scythe and his trusty lawnmower. He gears up to mow with goggles, hardhat and a bullet proof vest to protect him from flying branches, rocks, dog droppings and other hazards. Look for a cloud of dirt running behind a self propelled mower and you'll know you've spotted: BMX Dude!

Type Five: Neat Freak Dude

This guy doesn't want a lawn he wants a putting green. His grass is so beautiful, so uniform it looks fake with nary a twig or dandelion on it. He has an extra garage bay to store all of his lawn toys: hedge trimmers, weed whackers, blowers, edgers and snippers. He mows with the precision of a marching band strutting on the diagonal one week and then mowing in circles like a Zamboni the next week. Don't be surprised if you find the neat freak trimming his lawn with nail clippers.

Fortunately, the grass stops growing by the 4th of July in Steamboat Springs so wait to take your afternoon naps in late July.

As for me, I'm thinking about Xeriscaping.

Traffic Is Killing My Pie Obsession

Here in Steamboat Springs we have two seasons: winter and construction. After 19 years of living here, I've learned a lot about winter (layer, layer, layer) but until this summer I knew nothing about construction. After a few short weeks of summer I'd like to share with you my in-depth, comprehensive, no-holds-barred knowledge of construction.

Don't. Leave. The. House.

It's a monster truck rally out there! Yee-haw! There are massive dump trucks, mixer trucks, and semi trucks all grinding their gears down Lincoln Avenue.

The new Rocky Mountain High? Diesel fumes.

There's more orange on display now than during hunting season! Perky little orange cones dot the streets and orange signs that announce, "Road Closed" "Detour" "Flagmen Ahead."

Long-time locals pride themselves on knowing all the little short cuts, back streets and alleys where they can zig and zag to get where they want to go. Pronto. I even met a local who claimed he could go anywhere in town without making a left hand turn.

He moved.

I hesitate to give directions because familiar landmarks are gone. If pressed I find myself stammering something like, "Turn left where the old Harbor Hotel used to be which is now...uh...um...er...Olympian Place no, Howelsen Place or is it the Victoria? Well, anyway, you know, one of those new buildings."

Up until recently I've been pretty blasé about all the construction traffic. I tried to find creative ways to pass the time and entertain myself while waiting for the signal person to flip the sign from slow to stop. I keep a little notepad in the car to jot down interesting bumper stickers I spot. On my list:

- Girls Love Dirt
- Skier
- Free Tibet
- Must Be Pretty To Live In The City
- Shoot A Contractor Save An Elk
- *M* is for Mother Not For Maid
- Worst President Ever

- Money Talks. Mine Always Says Goodbye
- Hard Work Never Killed Anyone But Why Take The Chance
- Give Me Coffee And No One Gets Hurt
- You Must Be From The Shallow End Of The Gene Pool

That's fun for about a nanosecond. The most entertaining pastime is to watch, okay, spy on what other people are doing in their cars, either while driving or stopped in traffic. I've grown accustomed to people singing and, of course, talking on their cell phones. But texting while driving?

D-U-M-B.

For some reason people think they are invisible inside their cars. Maybe the dealer told them the windshield is really one-way glass and no one can see what they are doing. This has given birth to the car-as-bathroom phenomenon. The other morning a woman sped by me vigorously brushing her teeth. Other me-monkeys put on eye makeup, shave and file their fingernails.

Yuck.

The main reason why the construction traffic is getting to me is that it took me 15 minutes to get to Sweet Pea Produce and I was downtown when I started. I wait all winter for Sweet Pea to open, not for their produce (which would be too much of a shock to my sugar-addicted body) but for their pies. Late in February I start dreaming about their strawberry rhubarb pies (pies, pies, pies!) and I don't stop until the first forkful is in my mouth.

Let me just use this column to issue fair warning: If one more orange cone stands between me and my pie obsession there's going to be a trail of squished orange cones in my wake.

Watch out dump trucks. You could be next!

Having A Towanda Moment

Towanda!
This is the battle cry uttered by Kathy Bates in one of my all-time favorite movie scenes. Cut off from a parking spot by a car full of 20-something girls, Bates responds by punching the gas pedal, screaming, "Towanda!" and smashes into their car. Not once, not twice, but six times. Oh yes, the movie is *Fried Green Tomatoes.*

Now that I am...ahem....slightly older than the character in the movie, I occasionally contemplate a Towanda! moment.

Case in point:

Last week I arrived at the parking lot for tubers with three eager 11-year old boys. Everyone was anxious to get out of the heat and into the river. The only thing stopping us was a pack of 20-something girls in skimpy bikinis. There they stood blocking the one remaining parking spot. I rolled down my window, letting precious air conditioning escape, and stuck my wrinkled face out.

"Hi," I said brightly. "Can I pull into that spot?"

"Like, like, like, like, like, like, we're saving it," babbled the leader of the bikini brigade.

Clearly all of her exposed skin had given her sunstroke, a speech impediment, an unfortunate command of the English language, or all of the above.

I sighed. Patience is not one of my virtues.

"Well, I really need to park."

"Like, like, like, like, like, like, the car is coming."

A small growl began at the base of my throat. I looked over my shoulder and no cars were in sight. No police cars, no witnesses..... hmmmm....Towanda! or not? Feeling like the most boring, responsible, let's-not-set-a-bad-example mother on the planet, I put the car in reverse and began the search for a parking spot.

Once on the river, my mood improved. I bantered with other tubers- giving restaurant recommendations to a family from Kansas and chatting with another couple that wintered in the Bahamas and summered in Steamboat.

As I paddled along in the sunshine I contemplated the scars on my legs. Each scar a memory: a fall on a rock in Utah, knee surgery, a painful scrape along the cement trough of the Alpine Slide. All of these scars were surrounded by a constellation of black and blue marks and a crisscross of varicose veins.

Yup. My bikini days are over.

After a quick stop, I gave my big tube to my shivering son and his friend. They would sit up higher, out of the water, and stay warmer on my oversized tube. I now had to ride two tubes down the river.

At the next rapid, my tandem tubes flipped and I fell into the river.

Ping!

My elbow smashed into a rock.

Wham!

My butt bounced off another rock.

Ouch, ouch, ouch!

Elbow, ankle, wrist bumped against every sharp rock in the river. I struggled to keep my shoes on and my head above water as the fast current carried me along. My tubes, my son and his friends were nowhere to be seen but there were three older boys along the bank.

"Help!" I screamed.

To my complete dismay, two walked away.

Walked away! Were they too young to have seen, "Baywatch?"

On the brink of a near-death experience, I did what any woman would have done.

I thought about what I was wearing.

Yesiree. I started thinking about those 20-something girls in their barely-there bikinis. Would those boys have jumped in the river to save them? Probably. I reviewed my appearance. Ball cap, sunglasses, T-shirt, shorts. They probably mistook me for a lumpy piece of carpet instead of a damsel in distress. I threw my arms around a large rock and tried again:

"I need help!"

Finally, one boy who must have been an Eagle Scout and raised by a kind, compassionate mother, begrudgingly waded into the water to rescue me. I hauled myself out of the river and shook myself off like a dog. The next time I tube I think I'll wear a life preserver over my sensible L.L. Bean tankini.

And to any half-naked 20-somethings tempted to steal my parking spot, just remember what Kathy Bates said in the movie, "Face it girls, I'm older and I have more insurance."

Towanda!

Snoops Need More Scoop

The best daily entertainment in Steamboat Springs is the police record—a daily chronology of police, fire and ambulance calls. Admit it. I read it, you read it, we all read it.

What could be more entertaining, more diverting than learning about other people's problems? Finally a chance to be a bit of a voyeur, the nosy neighbor, or snoop you've always wanted to be. And besides, sometimes it's downright funny. Here are some oldies but goodies:

Pan of grease on fire!
Red blazer versus Ski Corp. sign on Mt. Werner Circle.
Woman yelling as if in pain on Broad Street. Officers determined it was a pregnant woman in labor.
Two lawn deer stolen sometime during the night.
11:05 a.m. Boy reports bike stolen.
12:10 p.m. Boy reports bike found.

But, but, but! There's not enough of it. The record gives just a snippet, a tidbit, a tiny morsel of what occurred and then leaves you hanging. Here's an example: *Theft was reported in the 1300 block of Memphis Belle Court. Police gave a warning.* What was taken? Why was it taken? What do you mean a warning? "Put back that flower pot, you schnook?" Why would they only give a warning, why not recover the property? We'll never know.

8:41 a.m. A suspicious incident was reported at 12th and Merritt. At that hour in the morning it's hard to imagine what could be going on. A ferret escaped from its cage? A fox peeked in the window? Wait! I've got it. Someone wakes up and to their absolute horror realizes there's no coffee. Gasp! They hop the fence, jimmy the lock at the neighbors and rifle through the cupboards until they find the coffee. A clear case of (drum roll please) Breaking and entering!

One day there were two entries like this:

9:05 a.m. A woman lost something somewhere in Steamboat. A report was taken.
11:03 p.m. A woman lost something in the 600 block of Snapdragon way.

Finally, a solution to my lost red kitchen scissors! I'm calling the police. I've been looking for them for months. And, yes, I already bought a new pair just to insure the old pair would show up, but they didn't. On a daily basis, I am broken-hearted I have lost these scissors. If the police would like to come over and look, they are more than welcome.

15

Bears also make the police record in Steamboat Springs. At this time of year, bear sightings pop up almost daily. Were they brown bears, black bears, honey bears? Did they growl, bare their teeth, show their claws? Was it a mama bear and her baby? C'mon now we need more detail than just: *"A woman saw a bear on Butcherknife Alley."* Was she 50 ft. away when she saw it? Was the bear foraging for berries? Did the bear think she was a berry?

Note to P.D. and editor of this very newspaper. We need more. Give us more, more, more! We want the dirt, the lowdown, the full scoop. Not this Cliffs Notes version of things. Give us the 4-1-1. Leave nothing to our imaginations.

We'd be happy with something like this:

8:10 p.m. *A noise complaint was reported in the 1800 block of Hunters Dr.* When police arrived they found a 42-year-old woman beating on her cluster mailbox and screaming, "My stimulus check from the IRS still hasn't arrived." Officers escorted her home, advised her to take a sedative and get horizontal on the couch.

P.S. If anyone finds my red kitchen scissors, please let me know ASAP.

Hunting for Groceries

Forget Department of Wildlife regulations. Hunting season really begins when herds of bewildered men begin foraging for food at local grocery stores. Watch them, clustered together at the end of every aisle, dazed and confused, eyes darting frantically in every direction--searching, hoping, praying--this will be the place where they bag their trophy: Red Bull! Eggs! Bacon!

Parking lots at City Market and Safeway resemble a four-color spread from the Cabela's fall catalog. Or a monster truck rally. Enormous diesel trucks, tote trailers loaded with four-wheelers, freezers, backpacks, tool kits, generators, winch chains, tow ropes, decoys, scopes, boots, maps, ammo kits, and, of course duct tape. Mysterious items bulge beneath tarps crisscrossed with bungee cords and ropes. These guys are good. These guys are smart. These guys know how to tie a knot.

Inside the store they employ the tried-and-true hunting strategy known as, "stalk 'til you spot." To aid in the search, they wear bright orange hats and camo to blend in with the cereal, bananas and ground beef. If you take your time and pay close attention you'll find them wandering the aisles like mice in a maze. If they can't find something on the list, they will not, of course, ask a grocery clerk for directions. Instead they prefer to yell to each other:

"Hey Chuck, where is the Red Bull?"

"Dunno, get Bill on the Walkie-Talkie."

"Hey, Bill is there Red Bull in your aisle?"

"Nah. I'm getting doughnuts. Ask George."

"George! George couldn't find Red Bull if it was in his back pocket. Remember how he got us lost last year?"

"Oh yeah. Four hours wandering in the woods, and then he shot at a tree branch that looked like the rack on a five-point elk."

Buying meat before you kill meat seems redundant. But hunters know how to do things I'll never be able to do. For example, they can set up a tent, a process which left me so pudding headed I bought a pop-up camper. In the harshest of weather, they can follow the trail of an elk herd simply by looking at broken branches, scat and tracks. If they're lucky enough to bag their game, they know how to field dress an animal and get it back down the trail. So why can't they find a can of Dinty Moore stew?

It's true, grocery stores are deliberately confusing. They must subscribe to the theory that the longer you stay inside, the more you'll buy. The milk is miles away from the cereal. The florescent lights are annoyingly bright. There are too many choices: generic, brand name and organics all scream for attention. Is it better to overdraw your checking account and live longer with organics or cheap out, die young and buy generic?

To eliminate the confusion and help these poor hunters I have a few suggestions for grocery stores in Northwest Colorado.

- Produce a topographical map of the store with coordinates to items hunters frequently purchase like toilet paper, energy bars and Gatorade and Red Bull.
- Serve complimentary bugle lattes in bright orange cups.
- Offer guided tours or personal shoppers.

Of course, hunters aren't the only ones who have a hard time in the grocery store. Just last Sunday I asked the check-out clerk if they were all wearing orange vests to set the mood for hunting season and Halloween. She calmly informed me the Broncos (whose colors are orange and blue) were playing.

Duh.

Warning Signs of Cabin Fever

If the four walls of your house seem to be closing in on you, and you can't remember the last time you smiled you may be suffering from cabin fever, winter doldrums, January blahs, seasonal affective disorder or all of the above. Symptoms of cabin fever include but are not limited to doubling the amount of movies you order from Netflix, tripling the amount of ice cream in your freezer and quadrupling your wine and chocolate consumption.

To find out take the following quiz (please use a number 2 pencil). If a pencil is unavailable, find an icicle.

If you circle "A" to one or more questions, throw your snow shovel in the dumpster and head for the closest beach.

1. After looking at the thermometer to discover it's minus 15 (never mind the wind chill factor):
    A. Throw the thermometer in a snow bank.
    B. Throw yourself in a snow bank.
    C. Cry and watch the icicles form on your cheeks.
    D. Buy a one-way ticket to Florida.

2. Have you noticed any changes in your weight?
    A. Dunno. The scale is in the snow bank with the thermometer.
    B. My sweat pants have gained 15 pounds, not me.
    C. Don't bother me, I'm eating.

3. Have there been any changes in your sleep pattern?
    A. Don't wake me up. I'm still hibernating.
    B. My dog won't let them change.
    C. I can't sleep because the snowplow wakes me up.
    D. I wake up a 5 a.m. with a strong urge to migrate.

4. When you think about mud season, do you:
    A. Weep for joy.
    B. Have the phone number for central reservations in Moab, UT on speed dial.
    C. Visit a tattoo parlor and have, "Beach Baby" tattooed on your forehead.

5.   In the nightly wine versus workout debate what triumphs?
      A.   I choose to workout over drinking wine 90% of the time.
      B.   Where is the gym?
      C.   You are on a first-name basis at every liquor store in town.
      D.   I moved my exercise bike into the liquor store.

6.   What is on your screen saver of your computer?
      A.   Picture of Tahiti.
      B.   Picture of Jonny Moseley crashing through the bumps.
      C.   Can't find my computer. It's buried underneath a week's
            worth of long underwear.

7.   Are you in favor of adding an anti-depressant to the city water
      supply?
      A.   No thanks; I have it in I.V. form.
      B.   No, I drink a quart of water from the Lithium springs daily.
      C.   Hurry up, what are you waiting for?

8.   When a tourist kindly and sweetly asks you for directions do you:
      A.   Kindly and sweetly give them accurate directions.
      B.   Tell them to get back on the direct flight they came in on.
      C.   Send them the opposite direction from where they're going.
      D.   Both B & C

9.   Have you been more irritable than usual in the past week?
      A.   Shut up, stop asking stupid questions.
      B.   My neighbor's pit bull, "Fang" cowers when he sees me.
      C.   FedEx is afraid to ask for my signature.

10.   What percent of your time do you spend on the computer looking for
      cheap flights to warm weather destinations?
      A.   I told you I can't find my computer!
      B.   None of the time.
      C.   What time is it?

11.   To ward off boredom do you:
      A.   Drive 50 miles to visit the newest big box store.
      B.   Lay prostrate on your heated floors for hours.
      C.   Watch reruns of Hawaii 5-0 while soaking in the bathtub.

12.   At 4 p.m. do you declare it:
   A.   Pajama hour.
   B.   Cocktail hour.
   C.   Dinner hour.
   D.   All of the above.

13.   What music is on your iPod?
   A.   Jimmy Buffet on a continuous loop.
   B.   Jimmy Buffet on a continuous loop.
   C.   Both A & B.

Steamboat Resume

AUGUST 1, 2008
Career Objective
A position in business management with an interest in sales and marketing.

Professional Profile
Committed to professionalism; highly organized, work under strict deadline schedules with attention to detail; have excellent written and verbal communication skills.

Profile
Henry Haskell is the former vice-president of sales and marketing for a Fortune 500 company. During his tenure, his 30-member sales force tripled sales in the Ohio valley, streamlined operations and partied like rock stars at NASCAR'S Nextel Cup. His impressive track record earned him top sales manager of the year in 2004, 2005, 2006. He was featured on the cover of the trade journal, *Where the Rubber Meets the Road* and will be featured in the 2009 edition of *Who's Who's in Business*. He is the past president of Rotary International, chapter president of Toastmasters, keynote speaker at the *Tires of Tomorrow* conference in Frankfurt, Germany. Henry is married to Henrietta and has a son, Horace (B.S. Biology, Brown) and a daughter Hortense (B.A. Education and summa glooma latte, Princeton.)

SEPTEMBER 1, 2008
Career Objective
A position in business management.

Professional Profile
A proven track record of success in sales and management.

Profile
Henry Haskell moved to Steamboat Springs in July 1, 2007 from Akron, Ohio. He started his career as a tire salesman for Tires, Inc and worked his way up to vice-president of sales. He led a 30-member sales force, tripled sales and partied like a rock star at the Daytona 500.

OCTOBER 1, 2008
<u>Career Objective</u>
A position in the hospitality industry.

<u>Professional Profile</u>
I can read and write. I can pass a drug test.

<u>Profile</u>
As a former member of the ski team for the University of Ohio, Henry Haskell moved to Steamboat Springs in July, 2007. For the past 10 years he and his family have vacationed in Steamboat. He recently sold his 8,000 square foot home in Akron, his Steamboat ski-in, ski-out condominium, and is living in Yurt-Ville, Steamboat's affordable housing complex, 23 miles west of Baggs, Wyoming. He traded in his Porsche Cayenne for a 1996 Subaru Outback.

NOVEMBER 1, 2008
<u>Career Objective</u>
A job.

<u>Professional Profile</u>
I'm a good guy and a hard worker.

<u>Profile</u>
A powder clause is important to me.

DECEMBER 1, 2008
<u>Career Objective</u>
Give me a job!

<u>Professional Profile</u>
All of this waiting is driving me nuts. I can't pass a drug test but I still think I can drive a shuttle bus for the mountain. I need a free season ski pass.

<u>Profile</u>
Henrietta ran off with the former steer-wrestling champion of Buckskin County. Horace is on Ski Patrol and Hortense has shacked up with some dude

she met at the Buckle Bunny Saloon. He wears tight Wranglers, a big belt buckle, drives a diesel pick-up, and has some problem with his lip. There's always a bulge in it and he spits a lot. His name is Clyde-Cody, I think. It's hard to understand him when he talks because of that lip/mouth problem. Horace has a ski pass, darn it, and I want one too.

December 5, 2008

I finally have a job! I'm working at Tires-R-Us mounting snow tires. Why do you locals wait so long to get your snow tires on? I qualify for a merchant ski pass! I work the midnight to 7 a.m. shift so I'll have the whole day free to ski. I am a little tired but I think after a nap in my Subaru and a latte at Starbucks I'll be ready to bust out some turns on Heavenly Daze.
See you on the slopes!

Construction Town U.S.A.

Steamboat Springs officially changed its name today from Ski Town U.S.A. to Construction Town U.S.A. Residents in an uproar!

Ladies and gentlemen, clamp on your hardhats and get ready. This summer the ground will tremble, dust will fly and the air will hum with the bing, bang, boom of diesel engines, power tools and hammers as countless construction projects begin. When it's all over--if it's ever over--we can have a construction bowl party downtown with street dancing and a bonfire from all the scrap wood. But first some suggestions:

- Free earplugs and masks should be standard issue for all residents.
- Retailers: Stock up on Ibuprofen, Carhartts, Coors, ball caps, and Styrofoam coolers.
- Reprint all maps and postcards.
- Kids: Set up lemonade stands at Fifth and Lincoln.
- Offer chair massage at construction sites.
- Extend happy hour.
- Bungee jumping from a crane can be a new summer activity.
- Rename the Alpine Slide, "Sawdust Chute."

Restaurants offering all-you-can-eat specials should rethink their policy. They should change their menu to offer items such as Ball Peen Burger, Hardhat Hash, Backhoe Burrito and Re-bar Risotto.

Just like the United Way fundraising drive, big signs on the courthouse lawn need to be erected. One sign for each project. Which site will be finished first? As each phase is completed another red line can be drawn. A non-profit needs to join in the fun and take bets. Call it a trifecta—a prediction of the order in which the first three projects will finish. Let's have an announcer on the courthouse lawn,

"With overtime for all, the Olympian is ahead. Sheetrock is done and the drywallers are standing by with buckets of paste, but wait….oh no, a lumber truck jackknifed on Rabbit Ears Pass. More bad luck—windows are on back order, putting Howelsen place ahead by a row of bricks! But wait, what's this? A stampede of seniors has taken matters into their own hands and strapped on tool belts. The dark horse, the Community Center, has edged out its competitors and finished the roof. Who---eee. Go granny, go!"

A construction command center needs to be set up and staffed around the clock with burly men drinking bad coffee from Styrofoam cups and munching on stale doughnuts. A large conference table overflowing with blueprints, Coors and chew will fill the room. Walkie-talkies will crackle with construction-speak:

"Billy-Bob, can you hear me, over."

"Roger that! Jimmy-Joe. Has the backfill been delivered, over."

"What's that? (crackle, crackle) No, not Beer-30, backfill, over."

At the command center a special Webcam will capture and transmit real-time traffic information. The site will offer a construction timeline (which we residents of Steamboat Springs won't take seriously until we know better), and video clips of the transformation of Steamboat Springs (which we will continually forward to our friends with the exclamation, "Look how we're changing! You won't recognize our town when you come to ski next winter.")

Click here for hints on how to keep the dust out of your home and office.

Click there for instructions on how to get through early weekend mornings of hammers banging. Click away to hgtv.com if all this construction is rubbing off on you and you must remodel your home *today!*

As two million square feet of real estate rises and construction workers join our community, remember to buy that boy at the end of the bar a beer, smile at the dusty fellow in line at the grocery store and share a joke with the grimy guy at the hardware store.

Whether we're Ski Town U.S.A. or Construction Town U.S.A., our warm, welcoming Western spirit is here to stay.

Chapter Two: Life At Home

Clowning Around

A mid-life crisis is a predictable rite of passage, like getting your driver's license at 16 and collecting Social Security at 65. Some people trade spouses. Others opt for a visit with their guru. Still others quit their corporate jobs to open a surf shop in Hawaii. I got an oversized red rubber nose, size 26 shoes, a wiggle-giggler and at age 46, decided to spend five days in LaCrosse, WI at Clown Camp.

Clown Camp is a month-long series of classes at the University of Wisconsin that began in 1981. Students trying out clown names like "Giggles" and "Gertie" willingly bunk in dorms with cinder block walls, cold linoleum floors and sagging mattresses. No one seemed to mind. We were too busy. Classes on how to make, throw and even take a pie in the face, how to spit water between your teeth and yes, even how to pull a rabbit out of your hat consumed all of our time.

Fun is always on the agenda at Clown Camp and no one needs a BlackBerry to schedule it. A fellow participant might arrive at breakfast in a curly green wig, shocking yellow and orange pants and a polka dot tie, anxious to try out a new joke, "Hi, I'm Clarabelle. What do you get when you cross a chicken with a bell? An alarm cluck!"

Co-Co Nut, a clown from Hawaii, who topped off her costume with a palm tree, took me aside to share an important tip, "Never shake anyone's hand." My puzzled look caused her to continue. "They'll get you every time with a gag."

Oh.

Late at night, clown campers crowded into any available room for "balloon jams" practicing the twists and turns for monkeys and mice. Every time a balloon popped someone would shriek, "It's pop-ular, get it? POP-ular?" (No one ever claimed clown humor was sophisticated.)

There's lots to learn at clown camp. Who knew there were three types of clowns? A tramp is a sad, hobo clown, a whiteface is a more elegant, frequently silent clown and an Auguste (Aw-goost) is most commonly associated with Bozo and Ronald McDonald. Each type requires different makeup, costume, character development and physical movement. At Clown Camp, clowns select courses that will prepare them to work in one of three settings. Caring clowns work primarily in hospitals and nursing homes. Christian clowns, perform in churches and Sunday school classes and 'regular' clowns get the laughs at birthday parties, corporate events, and company picnics.

Clown costumes come in two sizes: XXXXL or XXXXXXXXXXL. I tried on everything from gigantic patched pants with polka dot suspenders to baby doll dresses with petticoats. In the end, I settled on a cowgirl clown outfit. A poofy red skirt, star patterned shirt, vest with fringe, mismatched socks and big red "Mary Jane" shoes with green bows.

I joined the ranks of Bozo and became an Auguste. My name would be Pickles (to rhyme with Tickles.) Clown makeup takes about an hour to apply, starting with the lightest and moving to the darker colors. The upper lip is always painted white, never red. By just painting your lower lip red, and leaving the upper lip white, the red area changes shape making it possible to see and understand your expressions from a greater distance.

As every day passed, I gradually grew more confident in my ability to make people laugh. When I arrived home I taped the clown credo to my mirror. "Help me to create more laughter than tears, dispense more happiness than gloom, spread more cheer than despair. Never let me grow so big that I will fail to see the wonder in the eyes of a child or the twinkle in the eyes of the aged."

At mid-life, I could happily live with that.

A Dog's Life Is Good Enough For Me

In my next life I'm coming back as my dog. Kizzy is a 30-lb Bearded Collie with movie star good looks. She looks exactly like the star of "Shaggy Dog," the new movie with Tim Allen. She lives in a community where dogs outnumber people. Every day the local radio station broadcasts the breaking news from the dog pound, located on Critter Court. First, "The Dog Gone Pet Report," followed by "Adopt-A-Pet."

Kizzy is brushed daily, exercised exhaustively and sleeps an average of 19.5 hrs. a day. At Christmas, she will get a new red collar; I'll get the bill.

Kizzy's Paw-Pilot includes standing bimonthly appointments at the dog groomer for an oatmeal bath, paw-i-cure and trim. I haven't had a manicure in months. Kizzy has a sleek gray and white fur coat; my dark roots are showing. Her dog food is a delicate balance of real chicken and healthy grains carefully blended for optimum nutrition. My dinner comes from the freezer with instructions to remover wrapper and place in microwave for three minutes. When she's having a bad day I rush out to buy her a bag of Greenies to cheer her up. In the winter, her paw pads are sprayed with Pam so ice balls don't form. My winter boots leak.

On Monday morning as I clutch my son's school backpack, half-eaten banana, juice box, overdue library books, permission slip for a field trip, letters to be mailed, my gym bag and, oh yes, stuff I'll need for work, I gaze at my dog sprawled on the carpet. She has done dog yoga (doga), rolled in the snow and taken a few sensible bites of her wholesome breakfast. She has greeted neighbors in the parking lot, bristled at another dog and chased a cat. All this activity will soon require a nap on her monogrammed bed from L.L. Bean. This is when I look at her enviously and say, "Trade ya!"

Kizzy has friends she sees everyday in Poop Park, the empty field behind my house. I seldom find the time to get together with the girls for coffee. When I walk Kizzy, people stop to quiz me about her breed, age, and temperament and I do my best to be a good spokesperson. They pat her shaggy head, "ooh" and "ahh" over her good looks, and scratch her underneath her chin. My new blue Patagonia fleece goes unnoticed. If these dog lovers have a dog of their own, we stand politely by while the dogs lift their legs, sniff each other's private parts and talk:

"Hey, which one is yours?"

"The tired looking one over there with dark roots."

"Where did ya get her?"

"Oh, we met through a mutual friend. She thought she wanted a lab! Hah! Labs drool, Beardies rule!"

"Is she nice, the tired one?"

"Yes. I just wish she had a pick-up truck so I could ride in the back."

"She doesn't make you go to dog obedience school or anything like that?"

"Only once. It was called agility. I watched all these dogs going through tunnels and following their owners around like, you know, dogs. Forget that. I just jumped up on a chair."

After Kizzy finishes socializing, I take her home for another nap. The more I think about it, my next life seems too long to wait. I think I'll buy myself a leash and hope someone adopts me.

Soon.

The Seven Stages of Garage Sales

Stage 1 – Inspiration: Friday

Yes! A garage sale. Why not? The household budget is experiencing a petite deficit; closets are overflowing and clutter reigns supreme. In a moment of entrepreneurial insanity, I decide to pool my trinkets, trash and treasures with others and haul everything over to a friend's house.

Let the pitching and packing begin!

After 30 minutes it is painfully obvious I single handedly could have launched the shabby chic craze. "Shabby chic" is the term bestowed upon a trendy style of decorating. Garage sale finds are "reinterpreted" and strategically placed around a home and voila, you and your domicile are trés chic. That would describe the entire contents of my house. Other than my mattress, I can't identify anything that isn't second-hand.

Stage 2 – Perspiration: Saturday, 6:00 a.m.

Why go to the gym when you can bench press boxes of books, pots, pans and small appliances? Pump up that heart rate with leftover tiles, bricks and light fixtures from home improvement projects. Here's a cache of kitchen gadgets from short-lived health kicks that includes, but is not limited to a juicer, something that freeze dries fruit and umpteen water bottles. The hall closet overflows with a collection of "volunteer wear," coats and fleece with sponsor logos I have earned from various World Cups and other sporting events. I hang onto these primarily for houseguests who may not understand the concept of layering.

Let them freeze.

Stage 3 – Desperation: 7:30 a.m.

Where are those early birds? I'm cold, I can see my breath and my entrepreneurial zeal is waning. I try to warm up by merchandising, grouping my belongings into sections like "entertainment" and "cooking." The other sellers prepare by tying on aprons and produce bank bags full of change.

Stage 4 – Negotiation: 8:03 a.m.

A car pulls up. There's hope! As I rush to greet the first prospect I almost trip over that stupid fish, "Billy Bob Bass" that sings, "Don't worry, be happy." Maybe they'd like a warm "volunteer wear" jacket to wear while they shop? Hey, that's your color; I'll give you half-price on it. More people arrive parking haphazardly, spilling out of their cars with kids, dogs, and to-go mugs brimming with steaming coffee. They feign disinterest as they pick through my collection of salt and pepper shakers, Sponge Bob videos and chipped dishes.

"It's vintage," I say to one shopper considering the purchase of a cracked old suitcase.

"I just bought it for $4.99 and read it on the airplane last week." I whine to a woman who is questioning my 50 cent paperback price.

She stalks off.

Stage 5 – Elation: 10:22 a.m.

I take a bathroom break to count and tally my proceeds. Enough for a tank of gas ... hoo-ha!

Stage 6 – Collap-sation: 11:45 a.m.

I'm so tired I can barely move. My back hurts. I am popping Ibuprofen at an alarming rate. I cannot stomach another cup of coffee and yet I have to find the energy for the "bag and drag." Repacking. Ugh. A friend arrives with doughnuts. That will help. I throw what I can still lift into trash bags, and head for the closest thrift shop.

Stage 7- Reconciliation: Sunday Morning

If I subtract the price of the chiropractic adjustment from my gross receipts I'll have enough for 9.9 gallons of gas.

Sigh.

I don't even warrant a Ski Haus buck.

But, hey! I can still buy a lotto ticket.

Do Not Send Me a Postcard

Even though Hallmark has not officially recognized it, residents of Steamboat Springs know there is a certain week in winter where it is okay to be depressed. Blues Break—a dreadful seven-day period where certain people with frequent flyer miles, large amounts of money and jobs that aren't tied to the resort industry get to skedaddle out of town. Of course those of us left behind don't begrudge them this good fortune. We merely hope they contract food poisoning, have lots of flight delays and lose their luggage. If you are reading this column you are one of the people who didn't get to go anywhere on this school vacation. And so you are, like me, working and buying a set of earplugs so you don't have to listen to your friends tra-la-la about their exotic beach vacation when they return.

When not working, I tried to find things to do that might cheer me up.

I decided to be productive and get my tax stuff in order for my accountant. Despite the fact the mortgage company and bank sends me envelopes clearly proclaiming, "Important Tax Information Inside," they seem nowhere to be found. They could be buried inside a pile of newspapers, magazines, bills and papers I've been meaning to sort through for quite some time. I am motivated. I want that $600 the government is promising to send me. I want every penny I am due and so I go on-line to read up on tax deductions everyone misses. Boy, howdy! Lots of crazy, interesting things.

- False teeth!
- A Seeing Eye dog!
- Humidifier and the extra electricity to operate it if a doctor orders you to have one!
- Losses incurred at the roulette wheel if you declare gambling to be a hobby!

Is this better than a beach vacation?

No, it is not!

Time to purge my closet of clothes I don't wear and things I don't use. Once I get the receipt I'll have another tax deduction. The only problem is that I have to actually get in the closet. It's just ever so much easier to wash the same clothes over and over and pluck them off a chair in the bedroom every morning. On the third attempt, I manage to pry my closet door open enough to squeeze through it. The heaps and piles of socks and clothes is so overwhelming I declare defeat.

Is this better than a beach vacation?

No, not even close.

How about a movie? A movie guarantees a two-hour escape and popcorn. I went and saw, "Juno." It terrified me. It made me remember that teenagers drive, get pregnant and drive while crying and pregnant. It was about as honest a portrayal of teenagers as I've seen since I've been one. I decided to lock my son up for the next eight years.

Was this better than a beach vacation?

Absolutely not.

All right, all right. Hit the gym. Get those endorphins going and cheer up. If you watched the Academy Awards you may have noticed the sculpted arms many of the actresses had. There were so many of these well-defined triceps and biceps I started calling them, "Xerox arms." It was so unoriginal. So,"I-have-a-personal-trainer-and-don't-eat-refined-sugar-or-carbs."

Nevertheless, I must go to the gym and try to get those same arms. But on the way out the door I trip over my large box of Girl Scout cookies. Stay home and eat Girl Scout cookies or go to the gym?

Girl Scout cookies.

Is this better than a beach vacation?

No, but it's getting closer.

Celery Gimmicks

Scene One: Interior of darkened Steamboat Springs home. Woman lays on couch with shades drawn, a half-finished bag of potato chips, French onion dip, chocolates and a water glass full of celery next to her on the floor. Her cell phone is pressed to her ear as she listens to the following:

Thank you for calling the Celery Institute and Center for Overeating. All of our Celery Care Specialists are currently busy assisting other people with no will power. Please stay on the line and listen as our motivational music plays, "Stop In the Name of Health, Before You Blow An Artery!" Your estimated wait (no, not weight!) time is four minutes. While you're waiting, we advise you to jog in place until a Celery Care Specialist is available. Thank you for calling the Celery Institute and Center for Overeating.

Happy, Chipper Voice: "Good afternoon, Celery Institute. My name is Genuinely Happy Gina. May I have your name?"

Woman: "Mrmmmf. Sorry, I had a mouth full of potato chips. Name? My name? Chips. That's it. Miss Chips. I'm from Chattanooga and I drive a Chevy. And I love celery." (Muffled laugh and sound of hand in potato chip bag).

Genuinely Happy Gina: "Really? The caller i.d. shows your name is Joanne Palmer. How can I help you? And by the way, laughter is often the first sign of a serious symptom of overeating."

Miss Chips: "No, I'm Miss Chips. My identity along with my waistline has been lost. Mrmmf. Anyway, let's get started. There's only 15 minutes until lunch. Bless me Gina for I have sinned. It's been months since I've eaten anything healthy and I see no reason to start now. I blame the holidays. I blame the parties. I blame the weather. And I have to get up early to work and…and….and…..well, you know, I had to have a half a dozen of doughnuts just to get out the door."

Genuinely Happy Gina: "I see. Well, I am not a priest and therefore I can't absolve you from the mortal sin of excess. Didn't you read any of the newspaper or magazine articles we publish advising you to eat before you go to a party? That way you don't stand by the food table and choose all the wrong foods."

Miss Chips: "Of course, I read those. But honestly, would you want to be one of those people? Isn't it insulting to the hostess to stand there, sucking in your gut and taking twenty minutes to eat one carrot, oops, I mean celery stick?"

Genuinely Happy Gina: "I see your point. It would be rude. Now, according to my records it shows you live in Steamboat Springs, Colorado. Is that correct?"

Miss Chips: "Mrmmf. Ah, yes. The world class ski resort."

Genuinely Happy Gina: "So couldn't you undo some of the holiday excess by like, say, skiing?"

Miss Chips: "Um, yeah. Except my car is buried underneath six feet of snow, I can't see out my window because there's so much snow piled up and I can't get motivated to get off the couch."

Genuinely Happy Gina: "Sounds like they need to add some Prozac and caffeine to the water supply over there."

Miss Chips: "Boy, do they ever."

Genuinely Happy Gina: Did you know that celery has 'negative calories' - that means, the amount of calories in the celery is less than the number of calories used to digest it."

Miss Chips (maniacal laughing): "Great. A math problem."

Genuinely Happy Gina: You could find all this out and more on our website: CeleryandSticks.com. Log on and order our recipe book, "101 Ways With Celery Sticks."

Miss Chips: "I knew there'd be a gimmick! Gotta go! It's time for lunch."

Grouch Potato

Welcome to Steamboat Springs, home of the newest reality TV show, "Grouch Potato." In this first episode we will meet and interview several contestants to determine their grouch factor index. The grouch factor index is calculated using a complicated mathematical formula -- kind of like the one used for the caucus -- where factors such as amount of snow shoveled since December 1st are multiplied by the number of days spent on the couch instead of at work.

Other criteria are: relationships with friends and family (have *you* called your mother lately?) and number of ski days vs. number of sick days. Bonus points are available for the contents of the contestant's refrigerator. Fast food, fried food and junk food can catapult a contestant to the winner's circle. Subtractions will be made for leafy greens, organic food and soy-based products. The winner will receive an all-expense paid trip for two to Sun City, AZ.

"Wait! We seem to be experiencing technical difficulties with snow on the TV screen. What? Oh, I see, our producer says that's just the 371" of snow to fall in Steamboat Springs so far this winter. The strange thing is….hmmmm….let me double check before I say this, well, yes, snow appears to be falling into contestant number one's living room. Morose Mike, is a snowplow driver and three-year resident of Steamboat Springs. Ah, Mike, can you tell me why you have snow in your living room?"

"Yeah, there's no where else to put it. The City of Steamboat Springs offers a $500 daily incentive for employees to take the snow home. I'm making big bucks just laying here on my couch watching the snow melt."

"But you also have your windows open?"

"Yeah. I've given up shoveling. I figure it's easier to let the snow come in and melt inside on my heated floors."

"Isn't that kind of messy?"

"Nah. I pay my kid a buck an hour to use the Shop-Vac."

"Contestant number two is Depressed Daphne, a ten-year resident of Ski Town USA. Daphne, how long have you been on the couch?"

"Leave me alone!"

"Alrighty then, we'll try another question. How many days have you skied this winter?"

"I work three jobs. Now, leave me alone!"

"Okey-dokey smokey. On a scale of 1-10 how grouchy would you say you are?"

"6,9442 to the power of 10. You do the math. Now leave me alone!"

"Is there any one thing that will motivate you to get off the couch?"

"Yeah. When my Girl Scout Cookie order arrives. I cashed in my 401K and bought every box they had. I'm not moving from the couch until the doorbell rings."

"Contestant number 3 is Pessimistic Polly. Polly, not only are you on your couch you seem to be wrapped in bandages and look like a mummy. How come?"

"The medical community is trying to keep it quiet but I'm suffering from a new condition called polypropylene poisoning."

"What the heck is polypropylene? Toxic waste?"

"Long underwear, you city slicker! I've worn nothing but polypro all winter and because of that I've broken out into a rash….it's highly contagious and I wouldn't recommend touching anything in the house."

"Time for us to go. Thanks to all contestants for playing. Because of the depressed states of all three contestants we've decided to send everyone to Sun City, AZ. What do you guys have to say?"

"We're outta here!"

Six Words Or Less

Baffled by Sudoku? Confounded by crosswords? Here's something new to try.

Grab a cup of coffee, settle into your favorite chair and write the story of your life—start to finish—in six words. That's right. Six words. No more, no less. Sounds easy? It's not.

It all started innocently enough last Saturday night when a friend handed me a book, "Not Quite What I Was Planning." "Here," she said, "This is fun to read in the bathroom." The 218-page book is a collection of mini-memoirs by writers famous and obscure. As soon as I read one entry, I was hooked:

"A Sake Mom, Not A Soccer Mom."

Sake Mom was going to be hard to beat but I was ready to try.

The next day, a snowy Sunday, was the perfect time to lie on the couch and flip through the book for inspiration.

"Pack-rat cleans house, loses husband."

"I like big butts, can't lie."

"I wrote it all down somewhere."

"Rich in degrees and student loans."

"I'm the fine print; read closely."

"Fifteen years since last professional haircut."

"Brought it to a boil, often."

"On the seventh word, he rested."

Do you try to sum up your entire life in six words or just one aspect of it? I contemplated this at great length as I scrubbed chewing gum out of the dryer. This activity did not seem noteworthy, although, if the petroleum based product I was using to rid the dryer of chewing gum caused the dryer to blow up later in the day that could rate a word or two. But laundry is no excuse. It inspired another writer:

"Detergent girl: Bold. Tide. Cheer. All."

Lately my life seems to consist of too much of everything except fun. Too much work, too much laundry and too much negotiating with a soon-to-be-11-year-old about his growing, changing, and urgent list of wants and demands. After my son started badgering me for a studded belt and a body spray called, "Axe" I had to face the fact that he was growing up. Growing up and away from me! Interestingly, Axe has a six-word slogan, "Spray it and they will come." They, of course, meaning *girls*. Heaven help us, it's time to lock *all* the doors. And change the garage door code.

In college my six-word summary would have been easy:

"Study. Party. Eat. Study. Party. Eat."

Okay, I'll be truthful about college: "Party. Party. Party. Eat. Party. Study."

After college there was: "Travel. Travel. Travel. Graduate school. NYC."

I did a seven-year stint in the corporate world and then bailed on the Big Apple for a job in Steamboat Springs. "Ski. Work. Ski. Work. Ski. Work."

As a sleep-deprived new mother, I would have written:

"Exhausted. Exhilarated. Exhausted. Exhilarated. Exhausted. Exhilarated."

It was easy to sum up small sections of my life but trying to write about the whole shooting match was not working. I decided to write about the dog's life instead. Even though she doesn't talk it's easy to figure out what she's thinking.

"Feed Me. Walk Me. Feed. Walk."

I even came up with six-words for the dog that sounded like a haiku.

"Snow Tickles My Tummy. Treats. Treats."

After dinner, inspiration finally struck. Get ready! Dear readers, I will now share with you the six-words that encapsulate all 54-years of my life.

Drum roll, please.

"I wish we had ice cream."

Clock Changing and Quantum Physics

W hat time is it?
Is it new time or old time?

I've been asking myself these important questions a couple of bazillion times a day since we all dutifully, "sprung forward."

The advancing of a timepiece by 60 minutes throws me into a state of *time-nesia*. For days I bumble around the house, hungry at all the wrong times, looking at clocks that moments ago I'd determined were set correctly only to ask myself, "What time is it?" "Is that old time or new time?"

It's not nice to fool with Greenwich Mean Time.

It's also not nice to mispronounce daylight saving time. That's right. Saving is singular. Daylight *saving* time. Because it's hard to say and sounds awkward everyone adds an 's'.

The solution to this linguistic conundrum is to eliminate the phrase, "daylight saving time," in favor of "old time/new time." If you've ever tried to make plans to meet someone on the Sunday of daylight saving time your conversation will probably go something like this:

You: "Let's meet at the gondi at 9:00 a.m."
Friend: "Old time or new time?"
You: "I don't know. What time is it now?"
Friend: "7:30 in the morning and I haven't had my coffee yet."
You: "It's 6:30 a.m. here but I must have forgotten to change this clock. Let me look at my cell phone."
Friend: "How 'bout I see you in 90 minutes?"
You: "Old time or new time?"
Friend: "Just be there!"

Whatever the time, I am here to tell you there are two types of clocks. Hard to change and impossible to change. Some clocks are clearly labeled with helpful words like, 'hour' and 'minute'. Other clocks only have infinitesimally small hieroglyphics that require a flashlight and magnifying glass. The smaller the clock, the harder it is to change, but the easier it is to throw out. Unless it's attached to a kitchen appliance. Then you have to drive to the dump. Once you're in your car you might want to leave it at the dump too because the only thing easier than changing the clock in your car is quantum physics.

Strictly speaking, digital clocks should be changed from 01:59:59.9 to 03:00:00.0.

You figure it out.

Who decides these things? Where to address that letter of complaint?

We can shake a finger and blame it all on two men. Benjamin Franklin (who sometimes gets all the credit) and a British chap, William Willett. Benji, was the clever author of the catchy phrase, "Early to bed, early to rise, makes a man healthy wealthy and wise." However, Ben-baby did not practice his proverb. As an American delegate living in Paris, he stayed up late into the night playing chess. In 1784, he wrote a *humorous* essay, postulating how many candles could be saved if Parisians woke up a little earlier.

Ha-ha!

His essay went on to suggest rationing candles and the ringing of church bells and even the firing of cannons to awaken those sleepy-headed Parisians.

Mon Dieu! Le cannon!

The French found this all so amusing they immediately deported Monsieur Franklin back to America. (Not really, but I'm sure they thought about it.)

Everyone breathed a sigh of relief until London builder William Willett, penned the 1907 pamphlet, "Waste of Daylight." Willy's motive was golf. He wanted more daylight hours to sink that hole in one. He advocated, "advancing clocks 20 minutes on each of four Sundays in April, and retarding them by the same amount on four Sundays in September." Germany adopted the idea in 1916. The United States jumped on board two years later in 1918.

And so, what began as a joke remains in effect today.

Clearly, the last laugh is on us.

Ha-ha!

Together We Have It All

When we met, I was a divorced, menopausal clown with a five-year old son. He was a job coach training a special needs client to push shopping carts from the parking lot into Wal-Mart. For years, we'd lived in the same town of 10,000 people, shopped at the same grocery store and skied on the same mountain but had never met until match.com introduced us cyberspace.

I had vigorously rejected the idea of online dating. At 47, I knew my femme fatale days, if they'd ever existed, were over. Ever the romantic, I held on to the hope of meeting someone at a party, on the chairlift, or through a friend. But I could not deny the friends of mine who'd had great luck with online dating. While I was going through my hoops, he was listening to NPR and heard a segment about online dating. Intrigued, he held a digital camera six inches from his face and posted his profile.

After considerable thought, I listed my profession as, "children's entertainer." There was no need to elaborate that I clomped around town in size 26 shoes and wore a red curly-hair wig. He hoped to find someone who enjoyed playing tennis. After a few emails and a phone call we met for coffee at the bookstore on September 17th. He was early. I was on time. He wore blue corduroy shorts that I've never seen him in since and I wore a pink cotton sweater. Later, I later wrote in my journal, "He's cute! He looks like Nick Nolte with blue eyes."

Even though we were both, 47, his daughter was in college, my son in preschool.

"We're not exactly at the same stage in life," I said, grasping for the obvious. "You're free. Now is the time to travel and do whatever you want."

"Let's just see how it goes," was his easy reply.

And so we did. We hiked, biked and when winter came, skied. Slightly superstitious and afraid to do anything that might jinx the relationship, I never wrote his phone number in my address book. I quietly held my breath as one month turned into two, three into four. After we passed the six-month mark, I exhaled.

Even though I don't play tennis and he prefers TV to books, we share many things in common. We're both from the Midwest. We both share a deep and abiding love for starchy foods in all forms but particularly mashed potatoes, pasta and funnel cakes. We are unfailingly prompt, dislike self-centered people and are easily distracted.

Neither one of us has a sense of direction. There's no point taking a map because we can't read one. Up could just as easily be down. And so we get lost wherever we go--even if we've been there before. On Mt. Werner, he'll swear we're on Rolex when we're on Rainbow. Thanks to me, we once spent three hours attempting to hike around Pearl Lake.

But laughter is the glue.

He is, quite simply, the funniest person I know. Even in the middle of the night. Once in the middle of a hot flash, I threw off the covers, jumped out of bed, wailing, "I'm hot. I'm hot. I'm hot." Without missing a beat he lifted his head from the pillow and replied, "Getting a little vain, aren't we?" I laughed so hard I forgot all about the miserable hot flash. Recently my son, now 11, came into the bedroom and whispered in my ear, "Mom I can't sleep." Once again, awakening from a dead sleep, he responded, "But, can you sing?"

He's so wildly proud of his home state, Minnesota, he should have been governor. He's likely to argue his tennis heroes, Nadal, Federer and Roddick, are champions because they have seen Minnesota on a map.

He doesn't get angry or yell at me when I run out of gas on our way to the movies, grab the wrong ski pass, or even lock the car keys in the car with the car running.

I'm stubborn, he's steady. I may never get a dozen roses and he'll never have a girlfriend who looks good in a bikini. But a few years ago, when I was in the ICU and terrified, he used his hands to make shadow puppets magically appear on the wall.

There is a magnet on our refrigerator that says: "We may not have it all together, but together we have it all." I couldn't agree more.

Happy Anniversary!

The Beer Is Behind the Jelly, Dear

I'd like to announce my latest invention. A device so revolutionary, so state-of-the-art, so golly gee exciting that millions of women across the nation will thank my colleague, Dr. Von Fleaburg and me. Yes, ladies the good Dr. Von Fleaburg and I have solved a problem that has plagued women since the refrigerator was first invented in 1915. After hours, nay, days of tinkering in the garage Dr. Von Fleaburg and I have designed a GPS system with voice prompts for men who can't find the mayo, the mustard or the football-field size container of leftovers in the refrigerator.

Medical science has not caught up to me and my esteemed colleague Dr. Von Fleaburg yet, but after hours of observation from a hidden camera in my kitchen and exhaustive scientific research Dr. Von Fleaburg and I have made a startling discovery: It is not a man's fault he can't find anything in the refrigerator.

We now have scientific proof that due to synaptic overload in the sports center of a man's brain certain messages cannot be transmitted. I will not bore you with the technical details of our double blind study except to state the results in the simplest terms my scientific brain can muster: There is a light-paralyzing phenomenon which occurs when the refrigerator door is opened. The shocking burst of light actually paralyzes the synapses in the brain that impairs men's navigational abilities. They simply cannot tell right from left; up from down.

The poor dears!

Furthermore, this light paralyzes the muscles in their arms and prevents them from moving items in the refrigerator. The neurotransmitters, which might fire a message to the brain such as, "Move the grape jelly to find the beer," cannot function. Let me repeat: cannot function.

To make matters worse, the blinding light then freezes all leg muscles. This frightening occurrence prevents them from bending their knees to see if an item might be on a lower shelf.

The poor, poor, poor dears. It's a wonder they can get out of bed in the morning.

This light-paralyzing phenomenon is not limited to just the refrigerator. It also occurs from the light emitted by the television set which is the reason Dr. Von Fleaburg and I created the remote.

Anyway, I digress. Here is how our remarkable invention works: A small device attaches to the outside of the refrigerator. So men will be motivated to use it, the device is shaped like his favorite piece of sporting equipment: a pair of skis, tennis racquet, golf club, football, etc.

For example, let's say you live with an avid sailor. The GPS system is shaped like an anchor and attached to the outside of the refrigerator. Here are some scenarios:

Man: Where's the bacon?

GPS: (British accent) Ahoy Mate! It's on the third shelf to the port side of the mustard. The best way to get there is to and bend your knees just a bit and hope you don't capsize on your kiester.

Health Conscious Dieter: Honey, where is the low-fat tofu yogurt? I want to make a zero trans fat smoothie.

GPS: Tofu yogurt hasn't been invented yet, thank goodness. Let loose and go for the ice cream in the freezer.

Snowboarder Dude: Yo, bro'. Where's the leftover lasagna? Also need to do the Dew.

GPS: (in rap style voice) Jib don't jive and there you'll be. It's on the bottom shelf, there don't you see? Dude, the Dew is on the door. Grab some and high five your bro'.

There's still time to order your GPS for the fridge navigational system. If you don't like this invention stay tuned for our next one: a toilet seat that automatically closes.

My Knight in Shining Dungarees

Lois Lane had Superman, Guinevere her Lancelot and Rhett rescued Scarlett from a burning Atlanta. My shining white knight is different. Meet my rescuer: The Repairman. When he arrives in response to my 911 call for household distress, I imagine he will fall on bended knee and say, "At your service." He won't add, "Ma'am." With luck, he won't sport a backwards baseball cap and he definitely won't be chewing tobacco, gum or mulling over an argument with his wife that he needs to share. He'll run his fingers through his dark, curly hair and listen attentively as I describe my problem. His teeth, sheltered by a little awning of a moustache, will display no food. His gentle touch will guide me into a chair and he'll carefully remove my shoes. My hero won't dream of asking if the malfunctioning appliance is still under warranty or to find the instruction manual.

Like many fantasies, this one is reality based...in my washing machine. Drip. Drip. Drip. That small sound could only mean big trouble. For those of you unfamiliar with the Laws of Household Physics, Law #1865 clearly states that the smaller the noise, the bigger the problem, and the larger the bill.

"Mom," my son's voice, full of wonder, only deepened my apprehension. "It's raining in the living room." I dropped everything—groceries, school backpack, car keys, briefcase and run to investigate. Sure enough. A squall has moved into the northeast corner of our living room. The carpet is soaking wet and little droplets of water are steadily falling from the ceiling.

"Get a bucket," I yelled to my son as I sprint upstairs for towels. Before I reached the top, my repairman fantasy kicked into overdrive.

I become afraid to open the phone book because I might chip a fingernail. I throw my perfectly manicured hand to my unlined forehead and say, "I can't cope." Then I collapse. I am awakened from my fainting spell by The Repairman. He tenderly holds smelling salts to my nose, dries my tears with his monogrammed handkerchief, and utters the phrase I'm longing to hear, "I can fix it. No charge."

In reality, Chuck shows up. Chuck is bald. His T-shirt reads, "It's All About Me," and barely covers his beer belly. Chuck arrives as my son is dancing on the wet carpet and chirping, "Is this what it's like in the rain forest?"

Chuck quickly figures out that the hose to the washing machine had sprung a leak.

"But it wasn't even on," I wail.

"Rubber rots," Chuck says, and hands me the flashlight.

I silently hold it as he disconnects the hose and turns off the water. I find my tool box, take the doors off to the laundry room and carry them downstairs. While I mop the kitchen floor I listen to him describe the end stages of his father's illness who he says is, "circling the drain."

To his credit, Chuck gingerly removes the tiniest piece of carpet and positions huge fans in the living room. When he turns them on, the dog yelps and runs for cover; plants and papers become airborne and I have to hold on to the couch for support as Chuck shouts out the details of the Broncos last game. At the end, he hands me a bill equal to a mortgage payment and says he'll return "soon" to pick up the fans.

As I watch him walk away, I cry out, "Oh, Repairman, hear my plea. Get me outta here!" Whisk me off to a land where a soggy carpet is the prelude to a kiss, where chivalry isn't dead and bad things are set straight by a vast army of helpful hardware men. Swing into the saddle of that white horse and come quick. I'll be waiting, mop in hand.

Our Lady of the Perpetual Washing Machine

There's a place I go to worship every morning. The windowless room is quiet with creamy white walls. As soon as I cross the threshold a feeling of hope comes over me. Maybe today will be the day I triumph over dirt. I stand in front of my washer and dryer to make an offering. Plink. In go the new khaki pants I bought for my son. He didn't even make it to the car before the dog jumped on him with her wet paws. Pif! Paisley boxers. Mmmmf! Thick ski socks. Thunk! Camo pants, camo jacket, camo T-shirt, the fashion of choice for fourth-grade boys. As the water rises, I add detergent and make my plea, "Oh great Tide, please do what the ads promise. Get these stains out."

I'm weird. I spend more time in the laundry room than any other room in the house. There are only two of us, nevertheless I do at least one load of laundry every day.

I like to wash, dry, but not fold. From the dryer, the clothes go onto my bed. When it's time for bed, I move the lump to my desk chair. In the morning the lump returns to my bed. Eventually, I sort out my son's clothes and put them on top of his dresser. Every now and then our clothes actually see the inside of the closet.

Before I start a load, I love to inspect my son's pockets for the treasures he hides. Rocks seem to be a particular favorite. Even in winter he loads his pockets with pebbles, striped stones and occasionally a heavy round rock that bulges against the fabric. Cargo pants can hold lots of tiny Lego pieces, army guys poised for battle and candy wrappers. Sometimes I find screws, a baggie or an expired invitation to a birthday party stuffed in there. My pockets, on the other hand, hold utilitarian items like tissue, coins and maybe a scrap of paper with someone's phone number scribbled on it.

I am not a slave to fashion. I start the day in my warm dog-walking fleece. Unless I have an appointment with an actual human being, the fleece doubles as work wear. My son, however, at age nine is increasingly fashion conscious. The other day, I caught a glimpse of his boxers peeking out above his pants on the way to the car.

Me: "Ah, Peter, those pants are falling off you."
Son: (indignantly) "Mom! I'm low riding."
Me: "Yeah, well, ride right back into the house for a belt."
Son: "Mom! (stamps foot) I have to set an example for the 'mini-mes'

at school."
Me: "Get going."

Even the dog worships the laundry room. It is her sacred hiding spot, the den she retreats to whenever there's a thunderstorm or fireworks erupt. I know this because I came home one day to discover everything—laundry basket, detergent, spot remover, fabric softener—upside down or cockeyed.

The dog hair on top of the washer was the first clue. Next, I followed a trail of blood into my bedroom. There sat the four-legged tsunami that had blown through the laundry room holding up a bloody front paw. Scared of something she jumped on top of the washing machine, tearing a toenail in the process.

I have a deep reverence for my washer and dryer. I bow before them every morning. I'm not sure other mothers feel this way, but for those of us who do I propose a saint be named after us. I'd proudly wear her medal on a necklace and call her Our Lady of the Perpetual Washing Machine.

I Owe It All to Thin Mints

Once a year, millions of women sit in front of their televisions sipping a chilled Cosmopolitan, chardonnay or champagne as the Academy Awards unfold. There will be the usual glitz, glamour and grandstanding. The usual parade of impossibly thin women wearing beautiful dresses and Harry Winston jewelry. Jack Nicholson, sporting his trademark dark sunglasses and devilish grin will be front and center in the audience as history is made. My fantasy is just once, one woman will make the most memorable speech in the history of the awards. After she thanks her agent, the Academy and her archangel, she will say:

"I owe it all to Thin Mints."

In case you haven't noticed, it's Girl Scout cookie time. And in case you haven't visited www.girlscouts.org, many successful women like Barbara Walters, Carrie Fisher and Mary Tyler Moore were Girl Scouts and probably sold cookies. "Selling cookies," the website proclaims, "gives girls valuable life skills like goal setting, money management and customer service."

They're right. Once you've mastered door-to-door sales, anything is easy. Even Hollywood. As a former member of Troop 141 in Evanston, Illinois, I can speak from experience that twisting the arms of my parents' friends and going door-to-door to sell neighbors on the merits of Thin Mints was hard work. I can remember lying on the living room floor surrounded by towers of boxes, order forms and money, fighting back tears because I had more orders than cash. Selling Girl Scout cookies taught me that I was not cut out for a career in sales or accounting, green is definitely not my color, and my recent decision to hire a bookkeeper for my business was exactly the right thing to do.

I discovered right away that I am a right-brain girl. That I am independent, a self-starter and terrible at arts and crafts projects. To remind myself of this, I keep a paperweight I made during my scouting career. It has a black and white picture of scrawny me in my uniform. Since I'm tall I look more like the gangly green bean than a scout. The photo is off-center, the edges are jagged and it is a thing that only my mother appreciated.

I still have my Girl Scout sash in my closet. How could I throw it out? It would be like burning the American flag. I worked really, really hard for every one of those 16 badges. Harder still, apparently, was sewing them on. They are lopsided, sewn on with uneven stitches and big knots.

Although it is the 80th Academy Awards, Girl Scout cookies are celebrating their 90th anniversary. In the early days, girls baked sugar cookies with their mothers, packaged them in wax paper bags, sealed them with a sticker and sold them door-to-door for 30-cents a dozen.

Today, Girl Scout cookies sell for $3.25 a box and there are nine different varieties. Tagalongs. Thin Mints. Do-Si-Dos. Samoas. All Abouts. Thanks-A-Lot. Café. Little Brownies. Cartwheels. Lemonades. Wouldn't it be cool if they added two more flavors to reflect popular culture? I propose: Blog-A-Lots or iEat.

Thank goodness, girls don't have to go door-to-door anymore. They can set up a table at the mall or in the grocery store and stand behind their colorful cookie boxes. I don't pinch their cheeks and say, "Dearie, when I was a Girl Scout I sold cookies for 50-cents a box." I simply look at their hopeful young faces, buy as many boxes as I can afford and hope they are better at money management than I was.

I'm always one of the millions watching the Academy Awards. And I always hope that whoever wins will encourage young women to be true to themselves. That it's okay to color outside the lines. And it's really, really important to think outside of the box.

Unless, of course, it is a box of Thin Mints.

Real Estate Mogul, Not

When the going gets tough, some folks go shopping. Some people give it up to a higher power while others head off to see a shrink. Me, I open a bottle of wine and after the second glass, call a psychic.

Let me explain.

For the last six months, all I've heard is that it's a seller's market. No inventory; name your price. This seemed to be true. Houses were flying off the market in 48 hours, sometimes at more than the asking price.

Then I decided to put my condo on the market. As soon as the "For Sale" sign hit the ground, things started to happen.

The morning of my first home showing I awakened to discover a bear had gotten into our bear-proof dumpster. After carbo-loading, he recycled the contents on my front yard.

Bear Scat.

Bear Poop.

Bear Excrement.

Yeech!

In the 18 years I've owned my condo, has a bear ever unloaded in my yard? Nope.

At 7:30 a.m. I pulled on rubber gloves and cleaned up the hubcap-sized waste along with fast-food wrappers, plastic bottles and other trash the bear tossed around in the parking lot.

Fun!

Now time to clean and get ready for my first set of potential buyers. In a furious blaze of activity, I rearranged clutter so it looked important and the clutter that looked like clutter was stashed in my car, inside the stove and washer and dryer. I even made chocolate chip cookies and chocolate chip banana bread to leave for the realtor and her client.

I was exhausted, ready for a nap but there was nowhere to take one. It'd been so long since I'd sold a house I'd forgotten about the constant cleaning. I'd also forgotten about a little known condition that occurs as soon as you are under contract for a new house.

Two-mortgage-stress-a-phobia-itis.

Symptoms of this disease include but are not limited to: wailing and whining, calculating net worth of household items on eBay, checking family tree for rich relatives, investigating modeling opportunities for the dog, and a few too many calls to my patient and kind mortgage man.

A quick Google search on "two-mortgage-stress-a-phobis-itis" revealed a distressing long-term prognosis: binging on chocolate chip cookies and banana bread, an inability to talk about anything else, and in extreme cases, having to give up self-employment for a high paying job....next to impossible in Ski Town U.S.A.

This is when I decided to pour the second glass of wine and call my friend, the psychic. Let me state the obvious here. I am not a logical person. Early on in this real estate process a friend suggested I do a cost/benefit analysis to help me decide between two properties. Given the choice of constructing a spreadsheet or finding the phone number of a psychic, what would you choose?

I thought so.

A good psychic (not the kind found at a carnival or who has an 800-number) can cut right to the chase and give a thumbs up or down. Just imagine your mother blessed with divine power and no baggage and you'll know what I'm talking about. After 15 mins. on the phone, I felt better. She assured me happy endings were in my future. My condo will sell in a timely manner. I will not have to face writing a classified ad for the newspaper to make my condo sound like the one for you. Now selling! Won't last long! Act now, don't delay!

But just in case you're interested, it's still available.

Chapter Three: Life On The Road

Countdown to Departure

9:00 p.m. I'm caulking the bathtub. I'm caulking the bathtub because I'm leaving on a trip. I'm caulking the bathtub because if the plane goes down I will not have to worry about friends coming over and commenting, "She should have caulked the bathtub."

10:00 p.m. Caulking the bathtub, continued. The helpful hardware man said it was easy. He said something about a bead of caulk, wetting your finger and running it around the rim.

10:30 p.m. Dig wet caulk out of bathtub.

Did I mention I'm leaving on a trip? The alarm is going off at 4:00 a.m. and the taxi is picking me up at 5:00 a.m.

10:35 p.m. Caulking continued. Why didn't I take notes when the helpful hardware man was talking?

10:37 p.m. Fling caulk gun across bathroom.

10:45 p.m. Bake banana bread. I am baking banana bread because I am leaving on a trip. I am baking banana bread because if the plane goes down my friends will come over and need something to eat. I do not want them to open the freezer and see 17 black bananas in there waiting for me to find time to make banana bread.

10:48 p.m. Clean refrigerator and freezer. Throw out expired veggie burgers and all things organic purchased when I intended to start my health kick. Finish off chocolate peanut butter ice cream.

11:00 p.m. Pay bills. I'm paying bills because I'm going on a trip. I am paying bills because if the plane goes down and my friends come over they will not be alarmed I forgot to pay my Visa bill.

11:30 p.m. Clean caulk from carpet. The helpful hardware man forgot to mention if caulk gets on the carpet it is very difficult to get out. Light beige bathroom carpet is a very, very bad idea. Rubbing caulk on a light beige carpet leaves a very, very, very dark stain.

12:01 a.m. Realize shoes I planned to wear are at shoe repair store being repaired.

12:03 a.m. Cry.

1:00 a.m. Create a living will in three easy steps at www.legalzom.com. If the plane goes down and I am in a vegetative state and my friends come over they will know what to do with me. Put me in the bathtub.

2:00 a.m. Finish caulking bathtub. The line of white caulk is straight in places and lumpy in others but it is drying beautifully. Six loaves of banana bread are cooling on clean countertops. My suitcase is packed and I have found another pair of shoes to wear.

2:15 a.m. Set alarm and go to bed.

2:30 a.m. I forgot to shave my legs. I have to shave my legs because I am going on a trip. If the plane goes down I do not want to die with hairy legs.

2:32 a.m. I am standing at the bathroom sink shaving my legs. I can't take a shower or a bath because the caulk has to dry.

2:35 a.m. I am sitting on the kitchen floor eating banana bread. Why not? This could be my last supper.

2:40 a.m. Where is my clean underwear? I think I forgot to pack it. I have to have clean underwear because, well, you know why.

2:41 a.m. Sleep.

2:42 a.m. What is alarm is set for 4 p.m. instead of 4 a.m.? Double check.

4:00 a.m. Alarm goes off.

4:15 a.m. Jump out of bed and get dressed, tripping over dog.

4:17 a.m. Pluck stray chin hairs.

4:53 a.m. Taxi arrives early.

4:55 a.m. Stumble out the door and into taxi.

4:57 a.m. Did I unplug the coffee pot?

Travel Policies

I have a strict and long standing policy to never travel with luggage I can manage.

I have permanent indentations in my shoulders from carrying excessive weight. Even if I have one carry-on bag it's overflowing with clothes, books, notebooks and other miscellaneous items I'll probably never use, but have, "just in case."

I like to pack clothes I rarely wear at home-- clothes, which I don't particularly like or don't fit me quite right, pack up nicely in a suitcase. In the event of water landing, I'd hate to ruin a favorite outfit. As soon as I reach my destination, I immediately miss the oversized sweatshirt and ratty sweatpants I live in.

In the good old days, before the underwire in my bra and the gelatinous goo in my hair gel were considered bomb-building materials, I carried on items such as a small color television, electric typewriter, Chicago's famous stuffed spinach pizza, huge duffle bags, and dozens of wrapped Christmas presents.

During my son's infant years I frequently traveled with a stroller, port-a-crib, car seat, diapers, wipes, toys, sippy cups, snacks, two suitcases and a variety of things (some educational, some not) to occupy the little prince's attention at every waking moment.

If you ever want to experience what it's like to be invisible, borrow someone's infant (preferably crying), place screaming infant on your hip and start down the aisle of an airplane.

No one will look at you.

No one will offer to help you.

Everyone will hope and pray you are not in the seat next to them.

Sometimes people will even change seats to avoid you. I know this to be true because once while traveling with my son and the above mentioned accessories my mother was allowed to board the flight with me to help schlep some of my carry-on luggage. On her way out, she tried to elicit aid from this huge body-builder man in the seat in front of me. His torso barely fit into one of those Gold's Gym T-shirts and his biceps broadcast the fact that he could easily bench press the 727 we were seated on.

"Sir!" she said, using two hands to give his VW-sized shoulder a shake.

"Can you help my daughter with her luggage when the plane lands in Hayden?"

He, obviously smart enough to understand how futile it is to argue with a mother, nodded yes. As soon as my mother disappeared from sight, so did he. He moved to the forward section of the plane and never looked back.

For the next 20 hours I watched this man avoid me. Even my neighbor who was on the flight avoided me. A blinding snowstorm turned the nonstop two-hour flight from Chicago to Hayden into a travel extravaganza. The plane spent much of that time circling Hayden, refueling in Denver, and circling Hayden. I spent all of my time walking behind my son as he toddled up and down the aisle. All of the expensive things I brought (some educational, some not) didn't engage him. He preferred to pass the time pushing the call button for the flight attendant, unlatching and latching the tray table 8,342 times, opening and closing the window shade 8,343 times.

Finally, snowy Mother Nature dictated we spend the night at a hotel in Denver. After collecting my luggage I decided, just for grins, to weigh it.

66 lbs.

A new record for the Nervous New Mother Goober Book of Records.

Happy Camper?

The origin of the word camping is derived from the French word *campo*. It can be defined as: cramming-as-many-of-your-household-possessions-into-your-car-attaching-car-to-pop-up-camper-and driving-as-far-as-possible-from-your-house-only-to-reassemble-all-of-these possessions-in-the-dirt. Once completed I made this startling discovery:

I forgot something.

I was exhausted.

For a June weekend, I'd packed two ten-year-old-boys, one dog, spaghetti, bacon, eggs, fleece pants, fleece underwear, fleece hats, fleece pajamas, sleeping bags, ground beef, bug spray, hiking shoes, water shoes, flip-flops, rain gear, warm weather gear, coolers, block ice, fishing poles, nets, buckets, I arrived at the campsite and realized I forgot:

- Flashlight
- Matches
- My warm coat
- Fuel for the propane tank

"It's part of the adventure." I sang out to the boys. "This is roughing it."

"Really?" My son replied. "How come so many other people have satellite dishes on their campers?

"Oh that's not really camping, "I replied. "Besides, I did bring three first-aid kits, six bathing suits and eight bottles of suntan lotion."

"Great. What is there to eat?"

"Carrot sticks and marshmallows for appetizers. Then, spaghetti."

I love to walk around the campsites (because I couldn't figure out how to get my bike in the car after I have loaded it with gear) and see how other people are set up. Most people seemed able to set up the awnings on their campers, string clothes lines for drying wet bathing suits, put down a piece of carpet in front of the camper door. They'd figured out how to bring their bikes, boats and brains. I'm surprised no one had set up a pool table. They had postcard perfect campfires, red checked tablecloths with citronella candles burning brightly and seemed able to relax at the campsites in comfy lounge chairs. Sitting down looked like a lot of fun. But I couldn't sit down yet. I had to get fuel for the propane tank.

I made a run to civilization for propane only to discover my wallet was back at the campsite. Well, no wonder! I'd banged my head so hard dragging the propane tank out from underneath the camper it was a miracle I even walked upright. Back to the campsite to retrieve wallet, back to civilization, back to camper. Bang head again putting propane tank back. Now the hose thingy-ma-jigys had to be attached and tightened. This required a four-letter word I surely didn't possess: tool. I wandered over to a monster RV with satellite dish and threw my blonde-headed self at the owner's mercy.

Monster RV man trudged over to my meager pop-up camper and looked at the propane tank. He didn't really get the full experience since he didn't bump his head.

"Do you have a wrench?" Monster RV owner asked me.

Hmmmmm, wrench.

"What color is that? I have a yellow-handled thingy in the tackle box for pulling out fish hooks." I said.

"I'll be back with a wrench."

He left, also without bumping his head. Surprisingly he returned. He deftly reattached the propane by whirling and twirling the wrench. Then he left again. Now I finally had a chance to sit down, munch on a carrot stick and inspect my constellation of black and blue marks. One from banging my knee on the trailer hitch while loading car, one from tripping over a massive log the boys had put by the campfire, two bumps on the head and a few miscellaneous scratches.

Where did I pack the Ibuprofen?

Hair Mousse and Toe Cleavage

Cleavage!
I forgot to pack my cleavage!

These highly intellectual thoughts have been on my mind of late. I've taken a few trips out of Steamboat recently and after spending time in airports and the 'real' world I'm here to tell you every woman who is ready, willing and able is sporting cleavage.

Huh.

This is why it's good to get out and see what is happening on the other side of Rabbit Ears Pass. Although Steamboat gets a lot of publicity for record-breaking snow, it's never been touted as a fashion destination. While I have seen tourists try to navigate icy parking lots in stilettos, most of us get through the winter clad in head to toe fleece. *Vogue* magazine editors have never been sighted here, but I heard we made the fashion pages of *Sheep Herders' Gazette*.

Since I'm self-employed, I don't have to 'dress-up' for work and being fashionable seems expensive, uncomfortable and unnecessary—as long as I stay in town.

When I lived in Manhattan I had fake nails and a weekly glue and fill to keep them attached. During my days in the concrete jungle, I did spend time trying to volumize my hair with a blow dryer and a round hairbrush—until the unfortunate morning I over-moussed and got the hairbrush stuck in my hair and had to walk down the street to my hairdresser's.

In Manhattan a round hairbrush dangling from a person's head doesn't even merit a glance, grimace or a giggle.

There was a time I wore jeans so tight I had to lay down on the bed to zip them up. Once they were on it, all urges to eat were suppressed because all bodily organs were so compacted they were unable to function. I had a delusion that I looked like Olivia Newton John until I split the aforementioned pants on the disco dance floor one night.

But I was never into cleavage.

I have to say that until the cleavage craze set in, I'd not give any thought to participating in it. I think I have what it takes but since I finished breastfeeding it's hard to think about this part of my anatomy as anything more than a former lactation station.

Still there are other opportunities to be fashionable. French manicures are big, especially on the toes. Sporting a slogan across one's rear end appears to be popular. I saw, "Love Pink Forever," and "Candy." Nevertheless, I can't get enthusiastic about having a butt billboard. Uneven haircuts seem to be the rage. Personal grooming anywhere and anytime also seems acceptable. At 5:30 a.m. the woman next to me on an airplane trimmed her daughter's fingernails. Next she spent the 30 minutes applying her makeup that required numerous applications from a powder puff. At a certain point it was hard to tell whether more clouds were forming inside the plane or outside the window.

I have to confess to feeling so un-feminine, so un-hip, and so un-groovy that at the next airport I found myself in the Body Shop asking a girl half my age to put some eye makeup on me.

"What eye shade colors do you normally wear?

She looked startled when I replied, "None."

She went to work applying neutral tones and shimmery shine that were suppose to revolutionize my appearance. I felt a little more girly after that and able to make my connecting flight without fear of being nabbed by the fashion police.

I haven't given up all hope of participating in the cleavage craze. There is, just in case you're wondering, toe cleavage. According to the 'fashionistas,' only two inches of your toes are permissible to peak from your shoes.

Maybe I'll give it a try this summer.

Chapter Four: Life During The Holidays

Busted!

After an early round of trick or treating, my dear sweet ten-year-old son calmly announced:

"I'm getting a restraining order against you. I want you to stay away from my candy this year."

He wasn't smiling as he said this. In fact, he looked downright serious as he continued:

"100 feet. I want you to stay 100 feet away from my candy."

Stunned, surprised, and suppressing a giggle I asked how he planned to carry out his threat.

"I'll go to the sheriff's office and get one."

"Really? On your bike? Besides, I don't think they give restraining orders for chocolate. If they did, it wouldn't be so hard to diet."

"I can try."

"You think I'll trick you to get your treats? What kind of mother would do such a thing?" (These are the times that I wish a little halo would magically appear over my head.)

"You did last year."

"What a pumpkin-headed thing to say! Even if I did, it was only to save you a trip to the dentist. Besides, I'm innocent until proven guilty. Or I confess. You have no evidence I took a candy bar."

It's amazing what selective memories kids have. If I ask him to find his school backpack, he'll have no idea where he put it. But he seems to have instant recall for any minor transgression I have committed. In his mind, it is crystal clear that 365 days ago in a moment of weakness or temporary insanity I *may* (innocent until proven guilty or I confess) have reached my hand into his overflowing Halloween stash and extracted one little candy bar. He can also remember a day when he had to do chores or that six months ago I refused to let him have a sleepover at a friend's house. However, he conveniently forgets the hundreds of dollars spent on Lacrosse and ski equipment, not to mention Legos or his cell phone. Surely if he remembered even one of these things he'd agree I'm entitled to some candy.

I'll be the first to admit I am a card-carrying chocoholic. There are soccer moms, hockey moms but I'm the ultimate chocolate Mom, available on all holidays, especially Halloween and Easter. And when it comes to Reese's peanut butter cups there's not much I won't do to get one. Reese's has been my favorite candy bar for over 30 years—there on my thighs during good times and bad.

I will also admit that I am a wee bit over-involved with the downtown trick or treating, silently groaning when he gets a Tootsie Roll (sticks to my teeth) lollipop (ugh) or a Milk Dud (there's a reason Dud is part of its name). I am understandably overjoyed when the familiar orange wrapper of a Reese's plops into his plastic pumpkin bucket. I may have suggested once or twice that he make a second pass by the fire truck since the fireman usually hand out Reese's but if the truth be told maybe I suggested it a dozen times. With all of the costumes, commotion and candy who can remember?

On the other hand, maybe this restraining order idea has merit. Forget Weight Watchers, stomach stapling and fasting. Maybe if I was busted for my chocolate consumption and thrown into the slammer I could survive 24-hrs. without chocolate.

Hmmmmm......The Long Arm of the Law Diet Centers.

But first, they'll have to find the empty candy wrapper.

Did I Mention the Tiara?

Now that the last official firework has fizzled, the parade is over and barbeque grills are cooling I have only one regret from the 4th of July.

I have never been a parade queen.

The sad fact is I have never been a homecoming queen, prom queen, rodeo queen or even queen for a day.

I am a queen wannabe.

Think about it. Would you rather spend an hour, say, spot cleaning your carpet or:

- Wear a glittering tiara.
- Have subjects (read: children) do your bidding.
- Listen to cheers and applause of subjects.
- Look sleek and slim in your queen costume.
- Ride in the back of a red convertible smiling and waving.

Did I mention the wearing of a tiara? I think I did.

If I was ever lucky enough to reign as queen I'd be ready to execute "the wave." A true queen executes the wave in a seemingly effortless manner, but when you break the movement down it's not as easy as it looks. The forearm must be held straight. The back and forth rocking movement begins at the elbow and then in a seamless undulating motion progresses up to the wrist.

Let's try it. Ready?

Elbow, elbow. Wrist, wrist.

Repeat.

Elbow, elbow. Wrist, wrist.

It's important not to wave so vigorously that you jostle the tiara.

Did I mention the tiara? I think I did.

There is just one instance where I would be willing to forgo the queen title and settle for princess.

Princess Kay of the Milky Way.

I am dead serious. This is a tradition that has been going on since 1954 when Eleanor Maley was crowned as the first Minnesota dairy princess.

Princess Kay of the Milky Way reigns supreme for 12 full days at the Minnesota State Fair. The first official duty of the newly crowned princess is to bundle up in warm clothes and step into a freezing cold custom-made refrigerator to have her likeness sculpted in a 90-lb. block of Grade A salted butter.

The ultimate honor.

For almost two weeks, the princess and the 12 finalists—all carved out of butter—spin in a refrigerated display case in the Dairy Pavilion for passerbys to admire. I have traveled from Steamboat Springs to Minneapolis to pay homage to the princess in all her golden buttery glory and it's worth the trip. At the end of the state fair, the butter bust of the princess is packed in a box and sent home with her.

Sigh.

Even though I am a big fan of butter and I'm sure I could wax poetic about all things dairy my dream of being crowned Princess Kay of the Milky Way will have to shelved. Sadly, my schedule and my advanced years does not allow me to compete for all of the fun queen titles out there like Miss Olathe Sweet Corn or Miss Fluffy Rice. I'm going to have to follow in the royal footsteps of author Jill Connor Browne, creator of *The Sweet Potato Queens* and develop my own queen character that represents Steamboat Springs.

Miss Cow Patty.

Look for me next year wearing a luxurious sequined brown satin dress accented with a bovine-patterned belt and a silver boa. Miss Cow Patty will be carried down Lincoln Avenue on the shoulders of those hunky Rugby players while blowing kisses and doing the wave.

Did I mention the tiara? I think I did.

Labor Pains

Because it's Labor Day weekend it seems only natural that I write about labor which mean I can write about childbirth or jobs.

Hmmm.....

Both painful. Both hard.

Since, at last count, I've had 35 jobs and only one child, it's easier to write about work.

I've been a file clerk, waitress, meter maid, clown, photographer, property manager, receptionist, copywriter, marketing director, director of communications, yoga instructor, substitute teacher, promotion manager, resource aide, and freelance writer.

Phew!

I was fired from the first "real" job I ever had. The year was 1982 and I lived in Manhattan. I had been hired on by J.C. Penney's corporate headquarters to write newspaper ads for their fashion department. In a room the size of a football field sat 200 earnest, creative people, each with their very own cubicle and typewriter. Have you ever heard 200 typewriters zinging and dinging at once? Electric typewriters!

The writers had to walk back to a closet and retrieve an ugly dress, hook it on the wall of their cubicles and write a newspaper ad about it. All ads ended with the sentence in easy care poly/cotton, $29.99. The dresses were so awful the only way to write about them was to turn an ugly feature into a pun or a play on words. For example, my neighbor in cubicle-villle, took a plaid dress and wrote this headline,

Launching Plaids
These dresses really take off for fall

Twenty-five years later, I still remember that headline. This was creativity. This was genius. I was never so in awe of anyone in my entire life. Writing my own obituary would have been easier than writing about those dresses. I failed at being so clever. I hung the dress in my cubicle. I put a piece of paper in my typewriter. And then I sat. I stared at the paper. The paper stared back at me. I still sat. I sat so long it's amazing I didn't hatch an egg. I didn't go to lunch. Maybe I went to the bathroom. I just sat and stared for eight very long hours. Sometimes on a really inspired day I'd type, "in easy care poly/cotton, $29.99." I guess I thought the hum of the typewriter might inspire me to type more words. It didn't. At 5 p.m. I returned the dress back to the closet and went home. After three months they fired me.

Somehow after that I got a job at a fashion magazine writing more ad copy. This time I could write. The editor-in-chief of the magazine had a name like Squidgy and started all staff meetings like this:

"Ladies! Ladies! Let's get started. Has anyone gotten engaged?"

Inevitably someone would stand up, flash a diamond and then we could get down to business.

Every day of the three years I worked there I lived in mortal fear of committing a fashion faux pas. Fashion faux pas were discussed in great length in the ladies' restroom. The conversation would go like this,

Snotty editor number one: "Can you believe she wore textured pantyhose with that skirt?"

Extra snotty editor number two: "What was she thinking? It's a plaid skirt!"

Snotty editor number one: "Didn't she read the August issue? Textured pantyhose are out."

Extra snotty editor number two: "Did you see her lipstick?"

Since leaving that job, I've managed big budgets, flown around the country on business trips, sat in countless meetings, served on the board of directors and guess what?

I'd rather have a trust fund.

Happy New-Thanks-Mas-Ween

Happy New Year! Pop open that bottle of bubbly, settle down in front of the TV and get ready for the ball to drop in Times Square. What? It's only August? Yes, only August. But sadly, I already have spotted Halloween candy in one local store. The way I calculate it, in a few short days the Christmas merchandise will be upon us.

By the time you read this column, the start of school will be less than one week away. As soon as the pencils, erasers, notebooks and calculators are cleared from the shelves, the fright masks, plastic pumpkins and candy will appear. I like Halloween, I really do. I just don't need two months to prepare for it. And I really, really do not need any extra incentive to eat chocolate. I already have plenty of rationales at the ready.

- Missed parking spot? Why not have a chocolate?
- Stubbed toe? Have a chocolate!
- Feeling sluggish? Perk up with chocolate.
- Stuck on a column? Eat an entire box of chocolate.

Last year, retailers pretty much ignored Turkey Day. And why not? Thoughts of Squanto, Pilgrims and the Mayflower do not inspire consumers to buy flat screen TVs, cashmere sweaters and new MP3 players. And so, Thanksgiving and Christmas just sort of morphed into one holiday giving birth to a new word: Thanksmas. The day after Thanksgiving, or Black Friday, is supposed to signal the start of holiday shopping—but retailers started enticing consumers to buy, buy, buy as soon as Halloween ended. This year, faced with a sluggish economy, retailers are going to have to find new ways to get consumers to buy. How about guilt?

- Buy this or the recession will get worse!
- Buy this or your kids will devote an entire therapy session whining about the Christmas they didn't get what they wanted!
- Buy this or your government will never send you another economic stimulus check again!

Since we live in Ski Town USA, holidays are not part of the equation. The 10-day period between Christmas and New Year's is a difficult time to celebrate anything except the pleasures of overtime. Ski instructors, restaurant workers, shuttle drivers and especially folks who work at the airport, plaster a smile on their faces, gear up for the crowds and hope they earn enough in overtime and tips to take a vacation in April. By the time New Year's Eve rolls around, locals all are exhausted, crabby and ready for bed at 5:30 p.m.

Whoopee!

After considerable thought, I've come up with a solution: holiday consolidation. I propose a new holiday for all of us who live and work in resort areas.

New-Thanks-Mas-Ween!

Happy New-Thanks-Mas-Ween!

It's New Year's, Thanks giving, Christmas and Halloween all rolled into one and celebrated in one day. New-Thanks-Mas-Ween. After you practice saying it a few hundred times, you'll get up to speed. Think of the advantages. Less stress, less debt and fewer hangovers. No holiday crowds, no fights with the in-laws and no long lines at the post office. Best of all, it's eco-friendly! Your children will hate you, but Mother Earth will love you. All you have to do is pick a day, any day between now and December 31, to celebrate New-Thanks-Mas-Ween. Spare no expense, (remember, you are celebrating four holidays at once) and do it up right! Decorate a huge pumpkin with a few of your favorite Christmas ornaments, drape some mistletoe over your turkey, unwrap a couple of presents and sing a rousing chorus of "Auld Lang Syne." If family and friends think you're crazy, just tell them that's the way it's done in Ski Town USA.

Happy New-Thanks-Mas-Ween!

The First Fight of the Holidays Is With the Tree

The three wise men had it right. On the way to Bethlehem, they carried gold, frankincense and myrrh. They did not schlep a Christmas tree.

Who is to blame and how did it begin—this crazy custom of chopping down a tree and hauling it into the house? According to the Christmas Archive website, the origin of the Christmas tree dates back to the 7th century when an enterprising monk appropriated it as a teaching aid. He felt the triangular shape of the fir tree was the perfect prop to describe the Holy Trinity of God the Father, Son and Holy Spirit. By the 12th century it was being hung, upside-down, from ceilings at Christmastime in Central Europe, as a symbol of Christianity. (This technique still works well in a house with small children or cats).

On this side of the ocean, an epidemic of the big bad bah-humbugs was sweeping the country. Christmas was considered a serious holiday. Other than church, a law passed in 1659 made any observance of December 25 a penal offense. No presents! No parties! No fun! The party-pooper Puritans were undermined by the arrival of German and Irish immigrants. In 1846, the first case of Christmas envy was recorded after the *Illustrated London News* featured Queen Victoria and Prince Albert with their children standing around a decorated Christmas tree. Suddenly, everyone wanted the same royally perfect family tableau.

It's easy to look happy once the tree is inside and decorated. It's selecting the tree and grappling with the darn thing that's the problem. "It's the first fight of the holiday season," a friend lamented. "He's happy with the first tree we see, but I have to keep looking." Of course, not just any tree will do, it has to be the *right* tree. A perfect tree. A fluffy, green triangle with no gaping holes. The trunk must be ramrod straight. The top must have a spire worthy of an angel. Finding such a tree is easy. At a tree lot, I immediately get in the spirit of things because the temperature is identical to the North Pole's. I shiver, stamp my feet, shake snow from frozen trees, twirl them, and just before my child chucks a large snowball in my direction, I pay a large sum of money to someone inside the warming hut and tie it to the top of my car.

Fun!

Once, seeking a more authentic experience, I joined friends to cut one down myself. Although you may envision this as one of those memory-making experiences—fresh air, blue skis, caroling—all I really remember is shouting, "Look out below!" as the runaway tree shot down a steep hill like a snowy torpedo with me floundering behind it on skinny cross-country skis. Whether you buy one or cut it down yourself, only half the battle is over. You still have to wrestle the beast into the house and get it in the stand. Once inside you will discover one or more of the following problems: the tree lists, the needles are prickly, the needles fall off, there is a hole somewhere, you cut off too much from the top or the bottom, you didn't measure the height of the ceiling correctly and the tree is either too big or too small. Of course I am not drawing from personal experience when I write that most of these problems can be corrected with clear fishing line, duct tape and drilling tiny holes into the trunk to add branches.

Last year I gave up. I now have an artificial tree. It is perfectly shaped. The lights work, the branches are full, and the angel looks beautiful on top. I can admire it in all its fakey splendor and think, "How lovely are thy branches."

I am one wise woman.

Reduce, Reuse, Recycle, Regift?

R ecently, Yahoo! News announced the discovery of a new phenomenon. The news was so miraculously an AP press release was issued and an entire website was created to showcase it. The phenomenon? Regifting.

The website-www.regiftable.com proclaims that, "Regifting has become a phenomenon." Hmmmm.....right away I could tell some over caffeinated copywriter needed to have his or her creative license revoked. Phenomenon, according to my dictionary, is defined as, "mysterious and unexplained." Barring domestic phenomenon such as a good hair day, matching socks and the ultimate—not arguing with my son, true phenomenon are frequently offered up by Mother Nature: The Grand Canyon, Alpenglow. Meteor Showers.

As for regifting, there's nothing mysterious about it. The first recorded use of the word occurred during a 1995 episode of Seinfeld. George or Jerry uttered the word and 13 years later it is being billed as a phenomenon. I'm not convinced. Regifting is tacky, cheap and sometimes thoughtless. Don't believe me, visit the website. The site offers a forum where regifting victims can share their tales of woe:

Dick from Pennsylvania writes in:

"I received an engraved bottle of British Sterling cologne with someone else's initials on the sterling collar."

Lynn from Bellaire shares this sad tale:

"My daughter had a birthday party and invited her entire grade school class. One attendee brought a rather large re-wrapped, re-gift. It was a 6-piece toy set, previously opened with 3-pieces missing thus making it un-usable!"

Leah, from Pensacola, received a coffee mug and flavored coffee gift set. She was thrilled until she turned it over to find it had expired five years ago.

The website, created by the credit counselors at Money Management International (MMI) offers an unspecified prize for the ultimate regifting story, which in keeping with the spirit of things, might mean you walk away the proud recipient of a rock hard recycled fruit cake.

According to a survey conducted by MMI, more than half of all adults consider regifting acceptable. Further proof that I am behind the times came from the book by David C. Barnette, author of the *Official Guide to Christmas in the South Or, If You Can't Fry It, SprayPaint it Gold* "If you don't believe in reincarnation follow a gift bag around this Christmas."

Nevertheless, I maintain, regifting, especially in a small town, is not the best idea you'll ever have. It's too complicated, a veritable tangled web of lies. Consider this scenario. At an art fair, Julie buys what she thinks is a beautiful, handcrafted cheese board inlaid with mosaic mice. She gives it to her friend Amanda as a wedding present. Unable to return it, Amanda dutifully writes a thank-you note and places it on the top shelf of a closet.

One year later, Amanda, by now pregnant with twins, dusts off the box, rewraps it, and gives it to her cousin Bonnie. Bonnie is furious. She can't believe her cousin doesn't remember she is lactose intolerant and never eats cheese. She rewraps the garish cheese board as a shower present for her friend Janet. Janet in a hurry to get to the white elephant party at her office forgets to look inside at the growing collection of gift cards and spider webs and takes it to the party. She is surprised at the reaction her boss Julie has when she unwraps the box, and discovers the cheese board.

When it comes to regifting, it's not the thought that counts. It's whether you can get away with it or not.

Holiday Horoscopes

ARIES (March 21-April 19): Rewrap. Regift. Rejoice. You have found a home for the white elephant you got last year. Now someone else will have a toilet plunger that sings, "I'm Too Sexy for the Bowl."

TAURUS (April 20-May 20): You're bullish about finances but don't let your optimism lead you in the wrong direction. Instead pretend that you're worried about the economy like everyone else and use it to play Scrooge. It's a great excuse to shop at the Dollar Tree and plead poverty. Nobody needs to know about the half a million you've got hidden away!

GEMINI (May 21-June 20): You've been naughty. You've been nice. Which one is it going to be? After all you love to keep people guessing. But, let's face it you're hoping your honey has seen those car commercials where a new BMW ends up in the driveway with a big bow around it. For a gift like that you've got to play it sweet and passive, at least until December 26th. Go ahead, SMILE, it will be worth it! You can frown again after the holidays!

CANCER (June 21-July 22): With planet Rudolph moving toward the North Pole, you'd better stick close to home. You know how nervous you get when asked to consider relocation and the thought that Santa might ask you to circumvent the Earth in one night—well it's enough to bring back the hives so bad that your nose turns red! Drink cocoa by the fire and lock the doors against intruders; especially those carrying presents and wearing black boots.

LEO (July 23-Aug. 22): You know you're king of the jungle and you will win the debate over tinsel or no tinsel, twinkle or no twinkle, but there's no need to roar about it. Reserve your growling nature for the long lines at the post office, the crowds in the stores and missing packages. Bah, humbug!

VIRGO (Aug. 23-Sept. 22): You're feeling smug because you've had the presents wrapped (in wrapping paper bought on Dec. 26) since July. Wipe that smile off your face, drop 15 Twinkies into your blender, add a bottle of rum, and see what happens.

LIBRA (Sept. 23-Oct. 22): You are the peacekeeper, neutral in all situations. As soon as your sister-in-law asks, "Did you gain some weight?" remember your mantra: "Don't take the bait."

SCORPIO (Oct. 23-Nov. 21): Remember: living well is the best revenge. Go buy that plasma HDTV, curl up in cashmere, sip your Dom Perignon and beware the fool that knocks on your door.

SAGITTARIUS (Nov. 22-Dec. 21): If you are looking for a roller coaster ride full of loop-de-loos you'll find it this year in a house full of insane relatives. Uncle Charlie will be drunk and hanging from the rooftop as he pretends that Santa is coming to take him away to someplace better. Aunt Mildred is sure to ask for the hundredth time, "What did you do to your hair?" Your sister is due for a meltdown of epic proportions since her boyfriend was discovered having an affair with a Victoria's Secret model. Welcome home, Sag!

CAPRICORN (Dec. 22-Jan. 19): Last year you bought your wife Carhartt overalls big enough to fit an elephant. You thought them practical. This year you splurged on a mega flashlight knowing how afraid she is of the dark. You better learn how to run—fast—to the local jewelry store or prepare to sign the divorce papers come January.

AQUARIUS (Jan. 20-Feb. 18): Okay, so it's your time of year—joy to the world, love to all people, peace on earth and all the rest. Trouble is, you've got five dollars in your bank account and your boss keeps threatening to fire you. Instead of freaking out, fire up your creative abilities. Grandma taught you to crochet so haul out the yarn and get to work—then call everyone else a shallow, materialistic consumer!

PISCES (Feb. 19-Mar.20): You are torn between a petal pink peignoir and asking that money be given in your name for a flock of chickens to remote villagers in the Andes. The chickens win but you are first in line at the January sales to get exactly what you want in the lingerie department.

A Local Dedication

Dedicated to all locals who must work this holiday season.
I don't have space to list all of you but a super big thank-you to:
Taxi and shuttle drivers, housekeepers, concierges, front desk clerks, property
managers, wait staff, newspaper staff, ski patrol, cashiers, UPS & FedEx
drivers, and most of all, snow shovelers.

E very tourist
Coming to Steamboat
Liked Christmas a lot...
But the Grinch,
Living just north of Oak Creek,
Did NOT!

The Grinch hated Christmas! He hated it all
He hated the skiing, he hated the snow
He shivered and shook when it reached ten below
He hated the joy, the merry and mirth.
He hated the idea of great peace on earth.

The season was cold and heartless and mean
Wrapped in ribbons and bows he hated the scene
Tourists complained when things went awry
And greed seemed to glaze over every child's eye

For tourists there was pleasure, rapture, and joy
A smile and chocolate for each girl and boy
But down in the town where locals resided
Were stores to be tended and tours to be guided

The Grinch knew they worked with never a frown
For tourists, they said, must not be let down
So they gave up their Christmas Day
To bring in the dough
So other could frolic and roll in the snow

He wanted to be happy, he wanted to relax
He wanted to have someone bringing HIM snacks
Christmas is coming, it should be a cinch
But he'd run out of time and his bank balance was pinched!

To top it all off, he was sick, sick, sick
His head was all stuffy and he didn't give a flick
The tourists fly in and bring in the flu
That makes everyone in town go, "Achoo!"

His fingers were frozen and so were his toes
It's hard to stay warm when ol' Doc Winter blows

The snow coming down upon Christmas boughs
Kept Grinch at work with a shovel and plow
So into the night he worked and he slaved
'Til pop went his back!
And both his knees caved

As he lay there curled up and moaning his pain
His boss came to him and said, "Shovel again!"
"No!" said the Grinch, "This really bites!"
"I've slipped in the snow and my back is in spasm
I wish I could fly far from this Christmas chasm!"

A family of tourists spied the old Grinch
They said very sweetly, "You're in quite a pinch."
"So sweet Mr. Grinchy" they said with a grin,
"Come warm yourself, dear, at our little Inn."

"Merry Christmas," they said, "And to you a good night,"
"We're happy to save you from such a cold plight."
The Grinch, he then melted
And his eyes sparkled bright
And his heart grew two sizes larger that night

He resolved that moment before his situation worsened
That he would become a Christmas person

He called down to room service
"Bring me a feast!"
I'm ready to start this holiday season
And carve my roast beast!

A Lifetime of Guilt

In case you're already feeling guilty about New Year's Resolutions—that you didn't make or keep any—I have some good news for you. New Year's Resolutions are out. Passé. Bye-bye.

Instead the hip, cool, groovy new thing to do is embark on a spiritual quest by making a life list. A life list is a pact with yourself of goals you hope to accomplish before you die. These goals can be the simple old standbys: "lose weight, drink more water." Or a little more complicated: "run a double marathon with Swami Origami."

The good thing about life lists, or at least the ones I've read, is that they don't seem to be tied to how much money is actually in your checking account or how realistic or attainable it might be. For example if your goal is to visit the moon, feel free to write it down. Some people have very time intensive goals like build a house, earn a Master's Degree or become quadrilingual (isn't bilingual enough?). *Men's Journal* advocated adding to your life list activities like, "climb an active volcano" (why?) and "eat a living thing" (Ewwwww! Why?)

The bad thing about life lists is that instead of having a year to feel guilty about what you did or did not accomplish you have the rest of your life.

Phew, what a relief.

To make a life list you may need the help of a life coach. A life coach is a fancy term for a person that helps you set your goals and then holds you accountable during weekly phone calls. In other words, you are paying someone a lot of money to behave like your mother. If you need the phone number of a great mother, let me know.

The final step is to post your life list online at 43Things.com. This popular web site, with over a million members acts as a kind of on-line cheerleading group to help you achieve your goals. Popular goals include skydiving and oddly, "pull a prank involving 100 lawn gnomes." Still, the website proclaims a life list helps you live a richer life and that pondering your life list gives you focus and momentum.

It all seems so complicated, doesn't it? In the good old days you could just drink to excess, wake up with a pounding headache and then watch football. Now you get to wake up with a pounding headache and feel guilty you're not training for that double spiritual marathon or jerking lawn gnomes out of the grass.

Nevertheless, not wanting to seem like an old fuddy-duddy I decided to jump on the life list bandwagon and make one. In no particular order here it is:

- Heli-ski.
- Invent calorie-free chocolate cake.
- Raft the Grand Canyon.
- Dance the lead in Swan Lake. Once.
- Have a front row seat at the Academy Awards and look fabulous.
- Go to Tahiti.
- Spend a month in a small atelier in Paris with a laptop and unlimited money to shop and eat.
- Ride a horse every day.
- Have all writers and artists earn the same amount of money as football players and famous celebrities. (Note to *Steamboat Pilot and Today*: I now charge $2.5 million per column!).
- Always be upgraded to First Class.
- Wear a thong and look good in it. Once.
- Take my boyfriend to the U.S. Open and have front-row seats.
- Take the summer off and travel with my son.
- Have the memory and body of a 25-year-old with the wisdom of a 54-year-old.

Now that I'm done making my list, I'm exhausted.
I think I'll take a nap and then call my mother.

Chapter Five: Life with My Body

Memorandum

To: The Body

From: The Brain

Re: Mind-Body Connection

First quarter reports are disappointing. Productivity plummeted. Profitability is flat. Aerobic activity hit a record low.

To reverse this alarming trend the following memo reviews our organizational chart and outlines suggestions for improved performance of the mind-body connection.

Organizational Chart

Chief Executive Organ (Brain): The brain is in charge 24/7. The body reports to the brain. It is not acceptable for the body to have "a mind of its own."

Chief Financial Organ (Cerebellum): All financial decisions must be approved by the cerebellum. Impulse buying is no longer permitted. Sidewalk sales are forbidden. Sale catalogs must be thrown out upon receipt. Overtime is cancelled until further notice. Purchase orders must be filled out and approved by your supervisor 30 days **prior** to purchase. Annual revenue must double.

Departments

Accounts Receivable (Stomach): The HR department reports you have used up all of your sick days for the entire year during the first quarter. There have been numerous reports of "bugs". Limit contact with small germ-carrying children and please sign up for new monthly wellness program: "Taking Care of You."

The stomach will no longer growl and feign hunger 15 minutes after mealtime. Please cease and desist longing for chocolate after 8 p.m. as it keeps the human awake. Bathing suit season is almost upon us. Your compliance is mandatory.

Accounts Payable (Muscles): Muscles will comply with the brain's initiative. Muscles will not fake spasms, aches, "charley horses" or otherwise undermine brain's attempt at physical fitness. Muscles will be increased in size by 20% to handle expected loads. Please attend our brown bag lunch seminar: "Increasing Muscle Mass."

Human Resources (Heart): I am sorry to say there have been reports that you are trying to take control and act as decision maker. This activity will not be tolerated. You report to the brain. You are the HR department.

Cardio workouts are for your benefit. Do not have heart palpitations when you hear the word, "exercise." Also, clean out those arteries. Have a heart-healthy diet. Suggestions: use extra virgin olive oil. Eat avocados. Limit sodium.

Review and report all "longings of the heart" to CFO for approval.

You are required to participate in the sunrise exercise class: "Cardio Cha-Cha."

Security (Immune System): Please apply rigorous screening procedures and background checks on all potential applicants. Prospective employees such as infection, viruses and disease will not be permitted to work in this body under any circumstances. Check and recheck references and work history! Visit in-house library to check out, "Virus Vamoose!

Sales and Marketing (Liver): Overtime in this department has tripled. Hire necessary personnel and implement plan to process spirits more effectively and efficiently. Participate in weekly after hours business mixer.

Network!

Information Technology (Nervous System): Please maximize bandwidth of all synapses to improve firing of messages. Transmissions have been sluggish. This is an aging human we're talking about! Attendance is required at the weekend seminar: "Improving the Mind-Body Connection."

Thank you for your immediate attention to these matters. I look forward to renewed efforts across the body, improved productivity and profitability. Please plan to attend a mandatory staff meeting on April 1, 2009 to discuss these matters in further detail.

Remember our company motto: "A happy body is a happy human!

Dear Dictionary

Dear Merriam Webster,
Please excuse the large font but I can't find my reading glasses. I am also naked due to excessive body temperature. Wait! What was I writing to you about? Hmmmmm it will come to me in a min....let's see...spell check, oh good. Minute. Oh, I remember I want you to eliminate three words from your dictionary. The words are: Ma'am, menopause and middle age.

Ma'am/n.madam. Ma'am is a four-letter word. No one called me ma'am when I was 22. The word ma'am signifies men no longer see me as a siren but a senior citizen.

The first time it happened I looked around expecting to see some haggard old crone behind me and then realized they were addressing me. "Who me? Ma'aaaammm?"

Now not only do they think I'm old, they think I stutter. This slur is usually hurled by some waitperson with two chest hairs.

"Ma'am, would you like sourdough, wheat or Metamucil?"

This twit, not even old enough to know what life was like before text messaging does not need to know I can't read the menu because I forgot my reading glasses. This twit does not need to know I have shoes in my closet older than he is. All this twit needs to know is to drop the ma'am or his tip will suffer.

Menopause/n.1. the ceasing of menstruation. 2. The period in a woman's life when this occurs. A period pun in a dictionary? That may be the only laugh you'll get from menopause. Let me set the record straight. Menstruation doesn't just cease. I did not wake up one day to find a little illuminated sign flashing on my forehead with the message:

"Attention, menstruation is over. It's safe to wear white shorts and bathing suits."

No. First come the hot flashes. Remember the Indian sunburns you gave to your worst enemy as a kid? When you grabbed an arm and twisted the skin in opposite directions until they screamed? That's how a hot flash feels. These flashes can come in the middle of a meeting with your boss, while you're sleeping or during an expensive dinner.

No matter when they hit, you will suddenly have the insatiable urge to tear your clothes off and choke little twits who call you "ma'am" by twisting their head and body in opposite directions.

Middle age.n. The period between youth and old age, about 45 to 60. Here they go with that period thing again. I do not need the English language to tell me I have crossed the threshold into middle age. All I have to do is look at my body. Gravity is happening to it. Gray hair, age spots, bumps, splotches, dots, lumps, humps, and bulges are all happening to it. If I had the money, Botox, liposuction and collagen injections might happen to it.

My body's betrayal is apparently so noticeable that a complete stranger recently felt compelled to comment on my sagging body parts. When I emerged from the dressing room of a high-end boutique, a woman with a thick foreign accent approached me and said,

"You need a new bra-zzzziere."

The horrified look on my face didn't deter her. She continued,

"You know, lift and separate."

Clearly, the old gray mare ain't what she used to be. But, I've digressed. I must finish my letter.

Where are my reading glasses? Oh, Merriam-Webster guys, please ~~see~~ ~~agree~~ ~~to~~ DELETE these three words from the dictionary. Or beware! Indian sunburns from a lot of hormonally challenged women may soon be in your future.

The Fat Fairy Strikes Again

The Fat Fairy flew in last night.

She flits into my bedroom, sparkly wings creating the tiniest breeze. She wore a rhinestone-encrusted cape, pink tights and a tiara. She got right to work, pat-patting a new layer of fat onto my thighs. She never stops to talk. She's too busy (it's rumored she visits thousands of women a night.) If she ever did stop, I'd have a few questions for her:

1. Why me? Don't you have an enemy? Someone who stole your high school boyfriend? Cut you off in traffic last night? Infected your laptop with a virus?

2. Why my thighs? Can you please pick another body part? How about my big toe? An oversized big toe is fine. Or put a glob of fat on my ankle. Perfect. I'll wear socks. Earlobe fat, hair fat, elbow fat all fine, but no; she always flings her fat on my thighs.

3. How did you get your job? Was it posted on craigslist.com?
Wanted: one tiny woman able to fly while carrying a large bucket of fat. Must work nights. Must be able to ignore the sound of wailing women.

I imagine her in the interview, speaking in her little breathless voice "Yes, Fairy Devil-Mother, I feel my experience as CEO of LAR-DOUGH, Inc. is transferable and I'll be able to make an immediate contribution to your organization."

It's not hard to tell when the Fat Fairy has visited. As soon as I look in the mirror I know she's been here. Overnight my body has morphed into, well, ergh.... Shamu. My feet are still there, ankles fine, shapely calves, kneecaps intact but my thighs look like chipmunk cheeks, happily bulging with the pint of Double Chocolate Fudge Brownie ice cream that I'd slurped the night before.

The Fat Fairy does not travel alone. Like Thelma and Louise, Lucy and Ethel, the Fat Fairy has a partner in crime. She is the Dimple Diva (D.D.).

D.D. carries a bucket filled with a suspicious, smelly substance and a miniature garden trowel. Her goal is to make sure my thighs look like they sustained major hail damage.

The frequent visits of the Fat Fairy and D.D. have had a severe impact on the size of my wardrobe. I have eight pairs of jeans. They are:

- The Wistful Collection -Three pairs I used to fit into, but can't throw out because I may be able to get into them again. These live in the darkest region of my closet.
- The Stand-Up At Parties Collection - One pair I can't sit down in, or breathe in. Gives me a healthy flushed look.
- The Home Improvement Collection - One ripped pair full of holes and hanging threads. Perfect for stripping wallpaper or doing a wash and wax job on the car.
- The Height of Fashion Collection - Same as the Home Improvement pair.
- The Whoa Nelly Collection - One oversized pair of jeans I wouldn't be caught dead in because I'm *not* really that size.
- The When Are You Gonna Give Me A Rest Collection - One pair of L.L. Bean HAS IT! Stretch Jeans. Wear on a daily basis. These never make it into the closet. If I'm not wearing them, they can be found draped over the back of a chair, in the laundry basket or balled up on the floor.

Now that I only fit into one pair of jeans, I'm going on the offensive.

I've declared the airspace over my bed a "No Fairy Fly Zone." I'm sleeping with my son's Airsoft BB Gun and I'm not afraid to use it.

The battle of the bulge has begun.

Rest for the Weary

The problem with living in a Colorado ski town is that most everyone is a jock, thinks they're a jock, or tries to be a jock. Women have buns of steel, bulging biceps and zero body fat. Men come shrink-wrapped in little black Lycra pants, shave their legs and are obsessed with biking uphill. People around here like to sweat, except, alas for me. Sometimes I just like to sit down and do nothing.

Monday at 5:30 a.m. the lights are blazing at Health and Reek as locals begin their quest for the ultimate hard body. Rumor has it that some folks even have their own key so they can start earlier. Friends do yoga in lieu of lunch, sprouts instead of TV dinners and carob load on Friday nights to prep for a half marathon on Saturday morning.

Conversations at the supermarket, laundromat or post office are not about money, movies, and music. Instead it's all about how far, how long and how many. This "how many" conversation is one I could participate in if I was discussing my consumption of chocolate chip cookies (made with real butter). But my get up and go for exercise seems to have gotten up and left.

There is an unwritten local code of ethics that goes something like this: up is better than down; extreme is better than easy and ski until you drop is better than quitting before there's blood in your boots. The fact that the mountain is closed does not deter the hardcore local. They simply skin up, ski down, and head off to work.

Locals love to entertain around exercise. It's not uncommon to get an invitation to a party that begins with a snowshoe up Mt. Werner or a 10K up to the Hot Springs (note the invite reads up, no mention of down) followed by veggie chili at someone's house. No need to bring a change of clothes or go home to freshen up. It's perfectly acceptable to appear in fleece layers and smelling of l'air d'endorphins.

Eewwwww.

Sales of sporting gear in Steamboat Springs per capita must be the highest anywhere in the United States. Residents lucky enough to have a garage don't park their cars in them. How could they? Every inch of their garage holds rock skis, telemark skis, powder skis, shaped skis, last year's skis, this year's skis, mountain bike, road bike, fly rods, waders, kayaks, snowshoes, snowmobiles, shelves of water bottles, backpacks, a gross or two of Gatorade, Camelbacks, 619 Cliff bars and coffin-like cases for the top of their cars to haul some of this gear around in.

Woe is me, I don't have a garage.

Closets bulge with heart rate monitors, running shoes, jog bras, Smart Wool socks, polypropylene underwear, fleece socks, fleece vests, fleece jackets, fleece hats, Gore-Tex and neoprene.

A weekend getaway for ski country folks does not involve going to a five-star hotel, sleeping late and having brunch. It begins by driving half the night to a trailhead, sleeping in the car and starting out at 4:40 a.m. to climb a 14-teener.

I like to exercise, I really do. But I almost always have to go by myself, as I'm not able to keep up with half the people in town. I like to amble along looking at flowers and admiring the scenery. I'm not on a quest to get my heart rate up. And if the truth be told, this summer I'm daydreaming about a La Fuma lounge chair, a good book and a pitcher of iced tea.

There needs to be some rest for the weary.

Body by Bifocals

If you are looking for a new way to shape up for ski season, I have just the solution.

Buy a pair of reading glasses.

Owning reading glasses is the best low impact workout I've ever had. There is no need to worry about finding the time to workout because a constant workout. Ready? Here we go:

Squats: Bend knees 3,011 times to look under the bed, sofa and car seats for the pesky glasses.

Stretch: Stand on tip toes 2,021 times to search high shelves or other places glasses may be hiding.

Sprints: Double time up and down the stairs 32 times to look everywhere.

I am sure that Columbus discovered America, Sir Hillary conquered Everest and Charles Lindbergh traversed the Atlantic *all* in less time than it took me to find my reading glasses this morning.

Please do not suggest the obvious. Owning more pairs and/or wearing them on a "leash" around my neck will not increase the likelihood of finding them when I need them.

When it comes to reading glasses, logic does not apply.

Up until recently I enjoyed 20/20 vision. In elementary school I wanted to wear glasses so badly; I tried to cheat on the eye exams. I envied people who wore glasses of any size or shape and looked forward to the day I would join the ranks. Glasses, I've always thought, conveyed, an "I'm-a-smarty-pants-intellectual" look.

Imagine my excitement, then, a few years ago when I started to squint and hold things at arm's length. I quickly made an appointment with an optometrist. I was deeply disappointed when he uttered a word no woman ever wants to hear, "Bifocals."

I left and went right to the store to buy my first pair of reading glasses. Since then, a conservative calculation shows I have squandered at least one month's worth of my son's future college tuition on cheap plastic reading glasses. I have worked my way up the diopter scale (that's the magnifying level) from 1.0 to 3.0. However, if the glasses are really cute, I will buy the 2.5 and suffer a headache.

Other than not being able to find my reading glasses—at last count I think I had four pairs—there may be more but I can't find them—the other

Joanne Palmer

downside is that it makes it impossible to indulge in one of my favorite pastimes-reading in the bathtub. Bathtub reading is essential to my mental health. This is the place where I take my weekly 30 min. vacation to read *People* magazine. It's best to be in hot water to fully appreciate the trials and tribulations of Britney Spears and other celebrities. But now, sniff, sniff, and boo-hoo, bathtub reading is off limits until they invent reading glasses that don't fog or steam up.

Not being able to see presents other problems. For example, for the first time in my life, I ran out of gas. The little light on my dashboard read, "check gauge," but since I don't wear my glasses to drive—just to read—I drove around thinking it said "check gate." Even though the fuel gauge thingamabob was on 'E', female logic made it easy to assume it meant something else like, "Everlasting Gas."

Thanks to my reading glasses, I'll be the buffest middle-aged babe you'll see on the slopes, if I can only find my reading glasses before I leave the house.

Chapter Six: Life as A Mother

Keeping Time with the Refrigerator

It's hard to forget something you are reminded of 31 times a day. If my child reminded me of something that frequently I'd go berserk. But the Zen-like hum of my refrigerator is something else, indeed. That something else, frankly, is my hard drive. Truth is, my refrigerator organizes my life. Totally and completely. I've tried "Week-at-a-Glance," Post-it notes, and even a razzle-dazzle cell phone complete with calendar and calculator but nothing works as well as the low-tech door of my refrigerator.

The door holds my on-going grocery list, the school lunch menu, and inspirational quotes. My favorite by Emily Dickenson, "We turn not older with years but newer every day." It has a reminder notice for my high school reunion, emergency phone numbers and displays all of my appointments and a "to-do" list.

Two magnetized bins on the side are crammed with take out menus from local restaurants, receipts, bills, household budget, class schedules from the gym, and coupons, which I faithfully clip and fail to use. The door displays magnets that wonder where my hormones went, proclaim my status as a chocoholic and two that dare me to follow my crazy ideas. Every time I open the door to get milk I laugh at the cartoon that reminds me I'm under the care of two therapists, "Ben and Jerry."

According to an in-depth study conducted by, "Me, Myself and I" the average family of four opens the refrigerator door 31 times a day; 48 on weekends. This excludes holiday and diet periods when rates can soar. This means I am exposed to all my reminders 251 times a week—which is precisely the number of times I need to schedule an appointment to rotate my tires or schedule a bone density screening.

When I was single, I had no trouble carrying a planner and keeping track of my schedule. I exercised three times a week, remembered birthdays and got eight hours of sleep a night. I even flossed my teeth. My refrigerator door held concert and movie schedule, a list of food high in antioxidants, and my astrological compatibility guide. As a newlywed, the compatibility guide surrendered to decadent desert recipes and a list of romantic getaways. Once I crossed the threshold into motherhood, I discovered what all mothers know but medical science doesn't—all memory cells are destroyed during childbirth. New mothers carry planners that weigh 7 lbs. 8 ozs. and keep them up half the night. Reminders stuck on the refrigerator door are the only hope of getting somewhere in the lifetime you're suppose to be there. After a particularly maddening day with three children under the age of five, one frustrated mom I know posted her last will and testament smack in the center of her refrigerator door.

Interestingly, fatherhood enhances memory. New fathers never forget bowling leagues, poker nights or tee-off times. Their contribution to the refrigerator door will most likely be the stat sheet for the football playoff pool, a sale flyer for a new power tool or mulch.

Beware the individual with nothing on their refrigerator door. They suffer from a rare condition known as, "fridgafreakaphobia." They are under the misguided notion that the sole purpose of a refrigerator is to keep food fresh. The adjusti-temp shelves are perfectly positioned to maximize air circulation. They date and label leftovers, alphabetize condiments and arrange them in descending height order. These people should never be invited to join your potluck group.

Somehow in this jumble of magnets, paper, photos and bins I find whatever I need and get where I'm going on time. Since I've given up on plastering Post-it notes reminders on all available surfaces and just used my refrigerator door I haven't had an overdue fine from the library or the video store.

And my hard drive never crashes.

Dating and the Single Mom

When I got divorced, I thought about child support, custody, and my ability to weather the split, but I never once considered my dating. I just assumed it would happen-eventually.

A year passed. That's 365 days and what seems like twice as many nights without so much as dinner and a movie.

"I could fix you up with Killer," a friend volunteered. "It's just a nickname and he has a snowmobile." While contemplating how I'd ever introduce him to my mother, my son started waking up at 2 a.m. Instead of worrying about the haystack-size piles of unfolded laundry as I took the 16 steps to his room, wondering how will I ever have date or be intimate again when I might be interrupted by: "Mommy, I have a booger." Somehow, Killer didn't sound like the kind of guy that could handle it.

When I was single, I had a list of thirty-four qualities I was looking for in a man: tall, funny, successful, wants kids, and is a good dancer were some of the things on my wish list. Now I had a new list with only one criterion: can help a small child use a tissue.

I reversed my policy on personals and answered one. It read: "Take a chance on a decent, responsible man, 43. Non-smoker with a good heart." It was two weeks before we could get together. In the meantime we exchanged twenty-five e-mails, each revealing another detail of our lives. As soon as he got out of his SUV, he started complaining about the price of snowshoes, the price of the cheese he'd packed for our picnic, the cost of gas...you get the idea.

A friend counseled, "Just go slow and remember, it isn't you, it's every bit as depressing as it appears." My next blind date, a 6:30 a.m. breakfast, proved her right. Before I even sat down, he started reading the newspaper and ate two soft-boiled eggs without looking up, just like we'd been married for twenty years. It was, indeed, depressing—even if my married friends insisted I was lucky to sleep alone at night.

It was time to go on the offensive. I'd run my own personal ad. I hesitantly entered the newspaper office and began, "Communicative male...."

The woman on the other side of the counter began to laugh. I looked up and she laughed even harder. She grabbed a tissue and started dabbing her eyes as she said, "That's an oxymoron. Lemme tell you about my fiancé." I left.

I tried a party. When you live in a small Colorado mountain town, people think it's fun to have outdoor parties in the winter. I bravely stood outside in a blizzard, endured a blowing wind and smoke from a bonfire. After one hour, in the initial stages of hypothermia, I left. On the way out, the hostess said: "Why leave now? Bow-Wow-Chow the dog trainer I wanted to introduce you to isn't here yet."

I highlighted my hair and got a bikini wax. I strapped on ankle weights and did leg lifts. Surely rock-hard cellulite would counter the fact that I was a hormonally challenged, 48-year-old woman. It didn't work. The next date lasted just 20 minutes.

Desperate, I consulted a specialist in Feng Shui, the ancient Chinese art of paying someone to rearrange your furniture. She arrived in a black Saab turbo, her briefcase bulging with mirrors, bells and wind chimes. She placed a ba-gua (pronounced as if you're gargling) chart on top of a floor plan of my house. "I see the problem," she said in her clipped British accent. "It's the loo...I mean the toilet. It's positioned right in your relationship sector." I did as I was instructed: kept the lid on the toilet down and bought red bath towels.

The bath towels must have been the key, because my next fix-up was perfect—a New Age Nick Nolte look-alike. David burned incense incessantly and although he had no furniture he seemed to have an endless supply of CDs of monks chanting. Instead of working, he spent his day in meditation so I figured he could handle my consumption of EstroPause. But after a few dates, David announced he was redirecting his sex drive into his third chakra and left town.

Maybe it's time for Botox and a few more red towels.

Calling Detroit

Most mothers double as chauffeurs driving their children here, there and everywhere. We are forever running late, to Lacrosse practice, Winter Sports Club programs, racing across town to return overdue library books and making late night trips to the store to buy poster board for science fair projects due tomorrow. Mothers live in their cars, eat in their cars, change into ski clothes in their cars so why are car manufacturers so incapable of designing a "mom-mobile" that is both fun and functional to drive? Who cares about horsepower, turning radius or the transmission? We need a car that makes motherhood easier and it doesn't have to be pink. Listen up Detroit, I've taken a poll of mothers and have some ideas for you:

G.P.S. A global pie system is an absolute necessity for a mom-mobile. All road trips make me crave homemade pie and I need a navigational device to get me there. I'm talking about an old-fashioned diner that has big, beautiful pies spinning around in a clear case. Pies with flaky homemade crusts made from vegetable shortening and loaded with trans fats. I'm talking about a diner with a waitress named Betty who's smart enough not to ask, but just serves your pie "à la mode" with a steaming hot cup of coffee.

Privacy screens. At the push of a button, screens should cover the windshield and all windows so the driver or her passengers can change clothes in the car. Or breastfeed. Or take a nap.

Thank-You Light. After writing a big fat check you have a new alternator, but nothing new to wear to work. No boot cut jeans, new shoes or lingerie. And did anyone even say the magic word? A thank-you sign on the dashboard that lights up anytime you spend more than $200 on car repairs would be a nice feature.

Affirmation Station. Headphones for mothers only so they can listen to the words they most want to hear: "You are strong! You are powerful! You are thin! No, those jeans do not make you look fat. You are thin, thin, thin. Angelina Jolie has nothing on you, bab-ee."

Hypno-stick. A magic wand pops up, moves back and forth, back and forth, until small children in the back seat get sleepy, very sleepy and stop annoying their mother.

Central Vacuum. Naturally activates at midnight to suck up crumbs, dog hair and animal crackers.

Latte machine. Motherhood is exhausting but so much more fun with a grande mocha latte.

Aerobic Accelerator. Mothers always multi task so why not burn a few extra calories while driving to recycle? The driver's seat should double as a recumbent bike so you have buns of steel by the time you get there.

Aromatherapy Button. A light citrus mist to mask odors of dirty socks, sneakers and the wet dog coming from the back seat.

Subliminal Suggestion Station. The Barney song may be playing, but behind the music your children are hearing this message: "Mom is the most wonderful person in the world. Do everything she says. No fighting. Tell her what a great hair day she's having, and how much you love and appreciate her."

ATM Machine. Why drive through when the money can be right here, ready to go.

Recipe Cards. What to have for dinner tonight? Recipe cards at the push of a button, ingredient list faxed to the grocery store and ten minutes later Buff, the bag boy, is waiting curb side to load them into your car.

Detroit, thanks for listening. Let me know when this car is available and I and 10 million other moms in America will have our checkbooks ready.

Otherwise, I'm calling Japan.

So Not Cool

I am not cool.

I don't have tattoos or pierced body parts. I think my belly button is cute; I don't need to show it.

I've tried to be cool. I bought a pink Motorola Razor cell phone. It's cool but the operator isn't. I hate to admit it: I do not know how to text message.

I am not carrying the new, must-have $45,000 Luis Vuitton handbag. Whatever I need for the day fits nicely into a bag I bought at Ski Haus— partially paid for with Ski Haus bucks.

I've never downloaded a podcast. I have an iPod but it does not plug into my car radio. Speaking of radios, I don't have satellite, Sirus or XM radio.

I don't wear cropped pants or flip-flops. Since I'm tall that cropped pants thing makes it look like I can't find pants long enough for me. My feet are too ugly for flip-flops.

My son is cool-conscious. His hair is long. He no longer allows any PDA (public displays of affection.) He picks out his own clothes in the morning and prefers T-shirts with the logo of AC/DC or Green Day on them. We've started to fight over music. When one of two songs we both like comes on in the car here's what happens:

Son:	"Turn it up!"
Me:	"I like this song too. What do the lyrics, "soldiers dance for me, mean?"
Son:	"I can't explain it."
Me:	"Why not?"
Son (snorts):	"Mom you have to just *get* it. Hey, don't dance while driving. You're embarrassing me."
Me:	"Whatever."
Son:	"It's what-*ev*."

Whatever.

I have never watched an episode of *Desperate Housewives, Dancing with the Stars, American Idol,* or if it's still on, *Survivor.*

I don't have a home theater, surround sound or HDTV. In fact I had to ask my son what the initials meant (High Definition Television.) There's no

TiVo, plasma TV, just good old basic cable. According to my son, "There's nothing to do, nothing to watch, *nothing.*"

To prove how un-cool I really am here is an instant replay of a conversation I had after the first free community concert of *The Wailers.*

Me:	"Hey, how are you? Did you go to the concert?"
Cool guy:	"Yeah, it was a thumper."
Me:	"Uh-huh."
Cool guy:	"I recorded it. It was one hour 58 minutes and 15 seconds."
Me:	"Oh. I left early."
Cool guy:	"Oh."
Me:	"I didn't even think I liked reggae, but I liked this band. Especially the back-up singers in their green skirts. Boy, they could dance!"
Cool guy:	"Yeah, Bob Marley had a great band."
Me:	"Huh?"
Cool guy:	"Yeah, remember Bob Marley and *The Wailers?*"
Me:	"Really? No way, oh, no wonder. Thanks for telling me."

I don't own a BlackBerry, blog or listen to Beyoncé. I also do not have a MySpace page or instant message. I'm not going to camp out overnight for an iPhone. Even though I'm frequently lost, I have not installed a GPS system in my car.

I'm not cool.

And I'm cool with it.

Go Ahead Take My Day

Every seven minutes someone's identity is stolen. So--why did they forget me? If anyone would like to be me, I'll gladly give you my social security number, checking account number, the keys to my house and my banged-up, 1995 Subaru with over 100,000 miles on it. Here's a sample of what you'll get.

6:00 a.m. Alarm goes off. I have every intention of getting up, I really do. My plan is to get up and write a brilliant essay—something my writer's group will love. It's just that it's autumn, it's cold, and my son is in bed next to me due to a bad dream. I'm sure the clattering of the computer keyboard will disturb him so I turn over and go back to sleep.

7:45 a.m. Holy Snap! We're late.

"Get up, Get up, Get up! We overslept. We have to hurry!"

"Not my fault," argues my son sleepily.

I rush downstairs and put the coffee on. My son demands chocolate chip waffles for breakfast. In my haste I pour the batter in before the waffle iron has heated up. Disaster! I make peanut butter toast for breakfast instead.

"Let's go! Eat in the car. You don't want a tardy slip."

"Why not?" he quips. "I had 30 last year."

"Never mind, we're late. Feed your hamster and brush your teeth."

Somehow I get a glob of peanut butter on my bedroom slipper. As I race around the house picking up toys, newspapers, garbage I leave a trail of peanut butter behind. There's peanut butter on the carpet. On the bathroom floor. Everywhere I've been there's a trail of peanut butter.

"Lick this up!" I yell to the dog.

As I throw in a load of laundry, a furry face pokes out from behind the dryer.

"Honey, I'll feed the hamster later. Let's go!"

8:19 a.m. The Subaru roars to life and I race to the elementary school.

"Bye. Love you once, love you twice, love you more than beans and rice." I sing.

"If you did you wouldn't send me here," grumbles my son slamming the door.

9 a.m. Nurse calls to report I have an irregular Pap smear. That's all she knows. I have to wait to talk to the doctor.

"Am I dying or not?"

"Well, dear," she says in the saccharin voice many nurses seem to possess. "We're all dying. It's just a question of when."

9:09 a.m. Great. I may be dying but I have work to do. I'm a property manager, which means I know codes to every garage in town. Code 1102: Mow lawn, deftly circumventing the dog poop in the yard. On to the next house. Code: 1027. Winterize the garden. Cut, cut, cut all the sunflowers, day lilies, and columbine. Code 8686: Meet exterminator; feign interest in carpenter ants. Return to first house. Pick up garbage bag of grass clippings I forgot.

11:30 a.m. School nurse calls to inform me vision tests show my son is colorblind.

12:00 p.m. Head to health food store. Buy organic potato chips, organic chocolate bar and organic ice cream.

1:00 p.m. Add chemicals to hot tub. Code 1828: Flush toilets, disinfect bathtub, notice mouse droppings on Travertine tile. Code 2323: Meet deliverymen. Help haul in overstuffed chair and coach.

3:20 p.m. Pick up son and friend at school.

"Dude, we had a sub. She rocked! We watched a movie."

"Yeah, dude, my teacher is evil. Her hands are claws."

"Mom, do you know the Spanish word for penguin? Pingüino."

"Dude, can you show me how to get to Level 4 on Jack 6?"

"Mom, is God invisible? Like am I ever going to see him?"

"Dude you have to like die first."

3:22 p.m. "Mom! Slow down. Don't run the red light." Hmmmm, color blind?

4-8:00 p.m. Clean up peanut butter, coax hamster back into cage, eat macaroni and cheese, load dishwasher, empty dryer, throw trash in dumpster, walk dog.

8:30 p.m. Read *Alexander and the No Good, Terrible, Very Bad Day.*

9 p.m. Set alarm. Lights out.

My social security number is 441-21- oh never mind.

Who Wants To Be Frugal
If You Have To Be A Tightwad?

Frugality is not my friend. Trust me, I've tried. I drive an 11-year-old car, subscribe to basic cable and buy generic. Still, I once thought I could do more.

I started out by buying "The Tightwad Gazette." The author, Amy Dacyczyn, devotes 912 pages to being stingy. There's an entire chapter on dumpster diving. Pawing through garbage maybe Amy's idea of a good time but it's not mine. This frugal zealot also cheerily advises turning old credit cards into guitar picks and making volleyball net from six-pack rings. Amy reuses vacuum cleaner bags and can make a single roll of aluminum foil last for two years. When I got to the part about creating Halloween costumes by reusing the lint from your dryer screen I knew the book and I had to part ways. Besides I had flunked my initial attempt at frugality by buying the book instead of checking it out from the library.

A Google search yielded more suggestions (Miserly Tip # 18 "Rinse your hair with vinegar instead of expensive conditioner") and hundreds of frugal recipes. I printed Frugal Recipe #86. Mushroom-Onion Chicken. It called for 2/3 cup of French-fried onions that the author in Carrolsville, TX paid .79/can. Here that same can costs $2.69. Never mind.

Once gas prices soared over $3.00 a gallon, I decided to stop driving so much. Saving money this way was going to be easier than clipping coupons and buying in bulk. I'd seen "An Inconvenient Truth," Al Gore's film about global warming and discussed it with my son. I decided to ride my bike to pick my son up at camp. He already had his bike and I imagined the two of us riding back home along the bike path and maybe stopping at the Botanic Gardens.

As soon as Peter saw me arriving on my bike, a horrified look crossed his face.

"Damn Al Gore!" he wailed. "It's all his fault. I'm not riding home. I'm too tired and hungry."

I pleaded. I cajoled. I reminded him of the frogs he likes to search for by the pond in the Botanic Garden. I talked about building up his legs for ski season.

All entries were met with the same response,
"No!" "No!" "No!"

I'd like to say my arguments won him over. I'd like to say I remained calm. I'd like to say I uttered the Love and Logic one-liner:

"I love you too much to argue," and we merrily rode off.

But, no. Instead, I resorted to bribery. And that worked, but the cost of the bribe—a double-dip of bubble-gum ice cream, not to mention the bottle of Merlot I had to buy for myself cost more than the gas it would have taken to drive home.

The last time I tried to save money with a do-it-yourself home improvement project, the results were disastrous. Who knew sponge painting a bathroom could be so hard? First, I threw my back out bending over to pick up the paint can. No doubt the drowsy effects of the painkillers contributed to the final result—a Jackson Pollack! Great globs of Pepto-Bismol pink painfully commingled with a blue so blinding that the painter later had to wear sunglasses.

Spending money is consumer therapy but at least you have something to show for it at the end of the session. I'd rather read the comics than "Consumer Report;" squeeze the Charmin instead of pinch a penny. Financial experts always advise giving up your Starbucks habit and putting that mocha money into your retirement account. That's great, but how will you be awake enough to drive to the bank?

Pleasure has its price and sometimes I'm willing to pay it. Five years ago, I splurged and took my son to an all-inclusive resort in Mexico. There was 24-hr. room service, a concierge to cater to a tired mother's every whim and daily maid service.

Instead of diving in a dumpster, I dove for shells. At lunch when my son accidentally knocked the ketchup bottle onto the floor, shattering glass in every direction, the staff simply smiled and said, "No problema, senora."

No doubt, Amy would have picked up the shards to make a paperweight.

Losing My Mind

A few months ago, the World's Greatest Boyfriend (W.G.B.) and I were invited to join a potluck group. I love potluck groups. I couldn't wait to get out of my house, try new food and socialize. The theme: appetizers. An all-appetizer party. No desserts, no main course, just plenty of finger food.

The hostess had thought of everything. She had luminaries twinkling along the sidewalk, appetizers placed strategically around the room to encourage mingling and background music to create a festive atmosphere.

The W.G.B. immediately bonded with some of his fellow countrymen—Minnesotans. His body language indicated an instant replay of the Vikings last dismal performance on the football field.

I pursued a more intellectual exchange about the break up of Britney Spears and K-Fed while discreetly keeping an eye on the rapidly disappearing artichoke dip. Just as I was about to make a break for the dip I experienced the unmistakable symptom of my disease. Since a week had passed without a symptom, I'd half-heartedly hoped for a mini-remission. But after wondering why my pants felt so odd I finally looked down:

I had my pants on backwards.

"Moms-heimers!" I muttered under my breath.

At that moment, the W.G.B. appeared next to me.

"Whose-heimers?" he tried helpfully. "A beer?"

I slunk off to the bathroom.

The onset of this disease arrived exactly nine years, ten months and three days ago in the form of a nine-pound baby boy. As soon as I held Peter in my arms, memory cells started to explode, like tiny fireworks.

Pop! There goes the day of the week.

Ka-boom! Birthdays.

Pow! Grocery lists.

Zurrrr-zing! Phone numbers.

Poof! People's names.

I chalked up a misplaced diaper bag or forgotten appointments to sleep deprivation. But once my son slept through the night, things didn't improve. My dog's mournful face reminded me I hadn't fed or walked him. My gas tank always seemed to be on empty and oil changes were a thing of the past. Undeveloped film of promised baby pictures piled up until a grandparent threatened bodily harm.

Some things were decidedly not my fault. Am I to blame that Tupperware can't invent a universal lid? Is there a law that states Christmas *must* be celebrated in December? And birthdays on the actual date of the birth?

Once Peter started school, my already overloaded brain had to cope with the addition of parent-teacher conferences, fundraisers, picture day, school days off, homework and field trips. The collision of his schedule, school calendar, and my work life was a disaster.

"Look! A chance to have the playground all to yourself." I tried merrily when we arrived at school on Columbus Day, a school day off.

"You woke me up for this?" he whined from the back seat.

Friends suggested a supplement whose name my brain quickly transformed into Rocky Balboa. Try finding that at the health food store. I resorted to Post-it notes on my refrigerator door.

Since the potluck party, I've come to a few realizations. First, when it's my turn to host it, I'll do a pajama party and I won't have to worry about my attire. Second, since it will be nine more years before Peter leaves the house, I better get use to Moms-heimers. Last but not least, as long as I don't forget to feed him, pick him up and love him, I think we'll be okay.

Now where are those car keys?

Raising the Dead

When my son was little, he believed he could raise the dead. Distraught that his grandmother died ten years before he was born, he matter-of-factly decided he would bring her back to life. He assumed a Power Ranger stance—feet wide apart, shoulders thrown back, chest puffed out and said, "I'm gonna dig her up with my backhoe and breathe blood back into her veins. Then I'm gonna glue her hair back on. I don't know if I'm powerful enough but I'm gonna try."

I tried to explain she was in a happy place called heaven but he wasn't buying it. He badgered me to hop the next plane to test his four-year-old powers at a graveyard in Minnesota.

Dying scares me. It scares me so much that if I think about it—usually at night—I have to turn on all the lights and read until I can go back to sleep. Accepting death, I hope, will be like the concept of French-kissing. The first time I heard about it, I swore I'd never do it. Once I got older, it seemed like the natural thing to do. Maybe a time like that will come with regard to dying. At 54, it just doesn't feel like it will be anytime soon.

However when I think about my son dying, the lights are not enough. My throat constricts, my heart races and I have to sit beside his bed and listen to him breathe until I calm down. Every time I drop him off to ski I worry about a crash, a fall that will land him in the hospital. I already know that I'd be one of those in-your-face-top-volume mothers that cause doctors to think about early retirement.

Once he had to have five stitches removed from his chin. The skin had grown over two stitches and the doctor was struggling to remove them. They put him in a straightjacket type of device so he wouldn't wiggle and gave me two choices: either leave the room or pin him down. The doctor actually suggested I apply my full body weight to hold down my terrified, crying child. I snapped, "That will be a bonding moment!" glared at the doctor and stayed put to hold his hand.

My son articulates his feelings about death better than me. Two years ago, when our dog died, he was the only one who could describe the pain. He immediately said, "It's like a splinter in my mind. It's always there, it always hurts and you can't stop thinking about it."

Until Peter was born, I thought I knew what love was, but his arrival unlocked a fifth chamber of my heart. This tiny chamber bubbles with a wellspring of fierce unconditional love that's never ending. This love allows me to listen to him sing AC/DC songs in the car, allows my living room to be converted into a Lego laboratory and not to laugh when he complains about his "arch nemesis" at school. This love bursts with pride during mogul competitions and school plays. This makes me choke up on the first day of school as I watch him walk away from the car—a step closer to his future and further away from mine.

My son wasn't totally wrong about his powers, because he brings me back to life every day. He is my silly sidekick who frees me from the deadening world of adult responsibilities and commitments. He makes me laugh, he makes me sing, and he makes me forgo cleaning the house in favor of fishing at Fetcher's pond. He makes me realize that none of us can control how much time we live, but we can control how we live the time we have.

And most of all, he is a daily reminder that life, as long as we have it, is immensely worth living.

Dude, That Was Awesome!

According to the Second Edition of the esteemed Oxford English Dictionary there are 171,476 words currently in use in the English language. However, after a three-day holiday weekend only three words were used in my household: awesome, dude and I-need-more-fireworks (said with such speed it sounded like one word).

I-need-more-fireworks doesn't bother me. I only hear it for a week. I give him a budget and one trip to the fireworks stand and that's it.

However, I am tired of awesome and dude. Word weary. I am tired of them used individually. "Dude!" "Awesome!" I am tired of them used together. "That's awesome dude" or "Dude, that's awesome." Occasionally there are slight variations. Dude can sometimes be the second word in the sentence such as, "Seriously, dude, my fireworks were awesome." A pause. A look of panic. And then, "Dude...um...I...mean...Mom, I-need-more-fireworks."

No matter how they are used, dude and awesome annoy me as much as the sound of nails on a blackboard.

Screech!

When my 11-year-old son is with a friend they are incapable of starting a sentence without using the word dude. They look like two bobble-heads having a conversation that goes something like this:

Dude, what do you want to do today?

Dude, hang.

Dude, gaming.

Time out while Mom yells: "No gaming on a nice summer day!

Dude, how about going to the pool?

Dude, we need a ride.

Dude...um....I....mean....Mom, can you give us a ride?

Dude-Mom to the rescue again!

Awesome has become the standard response to everything, awesome or otherwise. Can't we give these two words a rest, usher them off onto the sidelines and welcome something new? Terrific! Wow! Fabulous! Awesome has been so overused it's lost all meaning. How awesome can something be if awesome has no meaning? According to the aforementioned esteemed dictionary awesome is an adjective meaning, "inspiring awe" or "excellent." Today, it is interchangeable. Awesome can be used as a response to any situation good or bad.

I took a gnarly bike ride today.

Awesome!

At the bottom I did an end-oh and crashed.

Awesome!

Got five stitches in my face and broke my leg.

Awe-soooome!

These two words need to be given a free membership in AARP, a one-way ticket to Arizona where they can play unlimited golf and enjoy retirement. Can't you just picture them down there in the heat?

Awesome: Dude, awesome putt.

Dude: Awesome, we can't say awesome anymore we're retired.

Awesome: But that's my name, dude.

Dude: Sorry. This annoying mother in Steamboat Springs got tired of us and sent us down here.

Awesome: That's so lame.

Dude: Careful, that will be the next word to go.

Awesome: But it was fun being popular.

Dude: You're repeating yourself. We just had that conversation last night with swell and keen. No one uses those words anymore either.

Awesome: What's going to happen to us?

Dude: Put on more sunscreen and quit worrying about it.

A computer makes it easy to get rid of a word. With one stroke I can zap it right into oblivion. If only it was so easy to delete words from the English language and my son's vocabulary. I guess I should be glad he's still talking to me, his dude-mom. In a few short years he'll be a teenager and I'll morph into enemy-mom.

So just to be fair I asked him what words he was tired of hearing.

Clean. Your. Room.

Touché!

Confessions of a Lacrosse Mom

I'm a Lacrosse Mom.

Before my son started playing Lacrosse, I knew nothing about it.

After the first season of Lacrosse, I still knew nothing about it. Oh, I understood there are sticks with little bird's nest baskets on the end of them. Shoes with cleats, hard rubber balls that have to land in the little bird's nest baskets, monster gloves, shoulder pads, an oversized helmet and a mouth guard. However, all of this scary-looking equipment pales in comparison to the most important piece of Lacrosse equipment.

The cup.

"I need a cup," my son declared one day.

"Okay. You have a water bottle, what do you need a cup for?"

"Mom, a *cup.*"

"I know. If you get thirsty just take a sip from your water bottle.

"A cup to protect my private parts!"

"Oh, a *cup.* Is that the same thing as a jock strap?"

"What is a jock strap?"

"I don't know, something boys wore when I went to high school. Call your father."

For those of you who have never seen a cup, it's actually shaped like the letter 'C' and when inserted into underwear designed to hold it the hard plastic shell offers complete protection for a young man's delicate private region. His father took him shopping for the all-important cup and we survived: "Lacrosse: the First Year."

Phew!

After a long winter, it is now time for "Lacrosse: the Second Year."

"Man up!" my son yelled to his friends before he headed onto the field. Man up? Man up! When did all of this testosterone arrive? Last year he did not scream, "Man up!" or "Man up, buttercup!" At least I understood the battle cry. I watched a practice that involved lots of running, guarding, pushing and catching the hard rubber ball in the bird's nest basket.

"It's like hockey," a friend tried helpfully. "They're two on two."

I pretended to understand what he meant but the only sport I really understand is baseball, which unfortunately, my son doesn't play.

Soon after the season began my son announced, "I need new Lacrosse gloves. These aren't steesy."

I thought for a minute and figured it was safe to assume gloves didn't have anything to do with his private parts.

"Ah, steesy? Can you translate?'"

"Steesy! It's a combination of style and ease. These gloves aren't steesy."

After much, um, ah, discussion (read: arguing) and a trip to look at new steesyier Lacrosse gloves he finally decided he could play with the ones he had.

Phew!

And so we enjoyed a few days of peace until we stopped at a friend's house the other day:

"Come in and see my Nutt Hutt!" he cried. With great trepidation I entered to see his fellow Lacrosse player swinging a pair of underwear over his head. In case you think I make this stuff up, let me assure you the Nutt Hutt is available locally and according to the packaging, the Nutt Hutt is the "perfect home for your most prized possessions."

The representation of the "prized possession" on the package is a tiny peanut in a shell. To protect this peanut, people are supposed to shell out (couldn't resist the pun) $40.00 for hi-tech underwear that promises extra ventilation, a reinforced waistband, superior range of motion and an installment loan plan for parents (ok, that part I made up). This cup looked large enough to protect the entire team and so indestructible that a Humvee could run over it without altering its shape.

What boy wouldn't want to strut his stuff in the Nutt Hutt?

Nevertheless, my son has not started to lobby me for the Nutt Hutt.

Yet.

I hope he waits until "Lacrosse: The Third Year."

I Yike Hammers

When I was pregnant with my son, I had great expectations. I'd whispered to my big belly, "You're going to hate math; love books." For months, I imagined the two of us curled up on the couch reading all the books I'd loved as a child—*Stuart Little, Charlotte's Web* and maybe even a *Nancy Drew*. There was no doubt in my mind he would grow up to be a sensitive English professor (with the smoldering appeal of Johnny Depp, of course.)

And then he was born.

Tipping the scales at an even nine pounds, Peter arrived loaded with enough testosterone to guarantee he and I would never spend time together at a poetry reading...unless it was the opening act for a tractor pull. He had a full head of hair and the appetite of a high school football team. The first time he nursed—two minutes after being born—he latched on with such gusto it replicated an experience I had previously only endured within the jaws of the mammogram machine. On day two, he refused to be swaddled in the sweet sleeper adorned with bunny rabbits in which I had planned to bring him home from the hospital.

At six months, he yanked the mobile off his crib and destroyed the black and white educational toy designed to stimulate neural development. Still, I reasoned, I had time. Maybe I had committed a terrible error by not playing Mozart to him in-utero, but there was no hard evidence to suggest he wouldn't grow up to prefer Hemingway to Hooters.

At 18 months, his first sentence, so descriptive and poetic, "ducky swimming in the water," sent my spirits soaring. I clung to my vision of him pacing his book-lined study wearing a cardigan sweater with leather patches on the elbows, fretting over the imagery in Hamlet's soliloquies.

I decided it was time to redouble my efforts to make him a literary genius. After all, I'd been an English major, surely there had to be one of my genes back-stroking in the pool.

I replaced his *Digger and Dump* truck book with, *Où est Spot?* We were regulars at library story time. I painted puffy clouds on the ceiling of his bedroom and brought home a Barney video devoted to manners.

On his second birthday, a friend gave him a plastic tool bench. He quit talking about duckies. His daily mantra became: "I yike hammers." His fascination with trucks and tools turned into a complete obsession. He had little interest in going to the park. He only wanted to visit construction sites.

"I go see the backhoe, mommy," were the first words out of his mouth every morning. I tried to interest him in my old Barbie doll. He took one look at her clad in her red evening gown and said, "I want to see her naked."

When I went back to work part-time, Peter went to daycare three days a week. Everything seemed to be fine until I arrived to pick him up one day. He was overjoyed to see me especially since he was in the middle of a time-out. The caregiver informed me that while changing his diaper he'd crowed, "Kiss my butt," I was speechless. It was then it hit me that our life agenda would probably include more home improvement projects than discussion of great books.

Peter is his own person; not the person I fantasized he would be. He's taught me that the reality is better than the fantasy. My pregnancy daydreams were black and white. He is living color. I've let go of my expectations and love him for the interesting little boy that he is. Now at eight, he wears camouflage pants and insists he wants to hunt. Yet the last time we baited a hook with a worm, he looked at me horrified and said, "Do we have to have a funeral for him?"

There's more to him then I ever allowed myself to imagine. He can be everything—tender and tough, sweet and stubborn—sometimes all at the same time. Recently, when the vet delivered the news that our beloved dog was terminally ill, I burst into tears. My son, threw his arm around my shaking shoulder, fixed the vet with a steely gaze and said, "We'd like a moment alone to discuss this." For his ninth birthday, he's lobbying hard for a BB gun and knitting classes.

Although math is his best subject, I momentarily stumped him the other day when I dropped him off at school. I said, "Love you 10 times a million, gazillion, trillion, billion."

There was such a long pause from the back seat I had to turn around. He rolled his eyes and said, "Exactly how much does that add up to?"

I think he knows it's a lot.

Chapter Seven: Life during Ski Season

I Say, "Right On!"

Recently, on an epic powder day, I skied with my favorite companion—a Snickers bar. I boarded the gondola with a group of guys who looked so young I calculated they had five chest hairs between them. The only woman, I felt old enough to be their mother. Maybe grandmother. The guys were staring at their boots, heads bobbing to the beat of the music coming through their headphones. We rode in silence until I couldn't stand it anymore.

"Hi!" I said brightly.

No answer.

"Great snow," I trilled.

One looked up. "Ummmmm. Ergh." He might have said, "Yeah."

I chattered on about the snow, how I planned to head straight for "Closet" and then I had finally had to give in to temptation:

"Don't you guys have girlfriends?"

"Ummmm. Ergh."

I took that as an affirmative and pressed on. "Why aren't they skiing with you?"

"Can't hang."

"Ah, what does that mean?"

"Can't hang. Takes them too long to get ready. Hair and stuff. "

"Ohhhh." By now we were at the top. "Well, have a great day."

"Right on."

Right on? I said that in high school. "Right on!" I knew what that meant. I think a raised right fist sometimes accompanied the phrase.

I'm afraid I've reached the age when I have to ask for the English language to be translated. At the start of the ski season, my son and I went to a local ski shop to pick up his season ski rentals. The technician, a nice looking young man, (maybe he had six chest hairs) seemed over caffeinated as he said:

"Here are your skis. If he lays the smack down, and needs something else, come back."

It was my turn to be monosyllabic. Ummmm. Ergh. What does 'lay the smack down' mean?"

"You know, if he's skiing really well and needs a high performance ski, come back."

"Gotcha. I mean, right on!" I tossed back over my shoulder as we left.

Fortunately, my son is fluent in ski speak and can help me. Last weekend we faced a sign outside the terrain park that read: "You want to huck like that?"

"Honey, what does huck mean?"

"You can take a lesson to learn how to do those cool, crazy tricks."

"No thanks."

I've learned the hard way that trying to keep up with children is not a good idea. A few years ago, a boy challenged me to race him on the Alpine Slide. Astonished, I accepted. I gave the sled full throttle and whizzed down, careening around curves, sailing over dips and drops until I could see the bottom. While trying to stop, the sled tipped slightly, scraping my right thigh along the cement trough. I won, but the road rash was not worth victory.

Still, on a perfect powder day, it's hard not to feel frisky. Short, shaped skis and two feet of soft snow made me feel like an adolescent instead of a card-carrying AARP member. I spotted a small jump and decided to go big. I prepared to be a huck-ette, hanging with the best of them. My smack down skis gathered speed on the descent and I got ready to soar. Instead, the tips of my skis augured into the opposite snow bank. I released out of both bindings and landed flat on my face. Poof! As I lay there wiggling my extremities to see if anything broke, I remembered why I only ski with a Snickers bar. Snickers can't laugh at you.

I also remembered the advantage of middle age.

I can afford a massage.

Right on!

Who Said There Are No Stupid Questions?

"Are you the consommé?" a brain surgeon asked the concierge at Steamboat Springs' most prestigious ski lodge. The startled woman looked up, and without missing a beat, said she'd prefer being called the soup de jour. And so begins the end-of-season-ski swap, sharing stories not equipment, among the people paid to keep a straight face when tourists ask funny questions.

Long after the snow is gone, locals are still regaling each other with can-you-believe-the-questions-they-ask-stories.

"When do the deer turn into elk?"

"How much is the $9.99 breakfast buffet?"

"What type of fish is a cilantro?"

"What should I do if I see a snow snake?"

"Snow Angels are members of Ski Patrol, right?"

Questions about the weather defy imagination. There is an assumption that every local has a direct link to the Weather Channel or a Snow God.

"When is the wind going to stop?"

"Will it ever quit snowing so we can ski?"

"Hey, let me give you Mother Nature's e-mail address," you're tempted to say. But life in a ski resort requires that you smile and pour the next round for guests who are constantly surprised that it is snowing while they're on a ski vacation. Or upset because it is a powder day. Or inquiring how a trail can be groomed if there's still snow on it.

Some of the toughest questions are directed at lift operators:

"Does this lift go up?"

"Which run goes to the airport?"

"Do all the gondola cars go to the same place?"

"Are my boots too tight?" a student asks a ski instructor who is required not to laugh while informing him that they are on the wrong feet.

"Where's my wife?" the gal at the Information Desk is asked. Interestingly, no one has yet to ask after a missing husband.

"Do you go to the Parmesan Inn?" a passenger asks a bus driver bound for the Ptarmigan Inn, a lodge named for the bird not the cheese.

Every so often the fact that we are a ski area is lost on people. An elderly woman calls in to insist she wants to travel by boat. "I want to take a ride on a steamboat! We'd like to start in Oregon and come back to Michigan."

Politely and sweetly she is told, "We aren't a steamboat, we are a ski area."

Moguls are also a source of confusion. "How are they made?" "Don't they come from Hollywood?" "Where do they store them in the summer?"

Maybe it's the altitude that causes visitors to check their brains along with their luggage. Maybe the Center for Disease Control should be studying causes and cures of Vacation Virus. Maybe we should, indeed, have a dress code that prohibits bathrobes. No one had even considered the need until a visitor asked the Maitre d' at a slope side restaurant if he could wear his to dine.

One local likes to tell about the license plate he wants for Colorado: "If you don't ski, don't bother." This is just his opening remark before he gets started on his imitation of the woman who asked, "Can we get a room with an ocean view?" Or the teenager who has watched too many Star War movies who wants to know if we frost the trees.

And so the next time the skier sitting next to you on the gondola asks about the big warehouse near Heavenly Daze tell him it's where we keep the snow in the summer. We'll be sure to put it all back next winter before they arrive.

The Four Stages of Winter

The thoughts, events and feelings depicted in this column are fictitious. Any similarity to any person living or otherwise is merely coincidental. Winter is not getting to me, it really isn't. However, any comments on this column should be forwarded to me in care of the Sunshine Sanatorium in sunny Phoenix, AZ. Did I mention sunny?

November 2007
Anticipation

When is it going to snow? Where's the snow? Why hasn't it snowed? Is it El Nino? Global warming? Great! The ski area delays opening. A sure harbinger of things to come. Guests are coming for Thanksgiving and there is no snow. Have I mentioned there is no snow? I am going back to bed.

December 2007
Elation

Snow is falling. It's finally here. Whoopee. Yippy Ki Yi Yah! Look at those lovely flakes, swirling through the air. It's white, white, white, white, covering up the dirty boring brown. I love living in Ski Town USA. Valley. El Nino-shmino. What do these weather forecasters know anyway? Zipadeedoodah!

Wow, still snowing and the tourists aren't even here yet. I make some turns today on my newly tuned skis and it's awesome. Man, can you believe it's still snowing? Forget sending Christmas cards, I have to get out there and ski. Ski, baby, ski.

Forget Christmas. I am not buying or wrapping anything. I'm too busy skiing. I have one more day until the direct flights land and I'm going to enjoy the powder.

I missed a few powder days because I'm working, but it's Christmas week and who wants to ski anyway? Too many people are here. I'll wait until they all leave and then the slopes will be mine. My back hurts from shoveling anyway. Hurry up holidays and be over.

January 2008
Frustration

It sure would be nice to see the sun but that's ok. I'm going skiing. Ski. Ski. Ski. Huck. Jump. Jib. Jive. Jam. Wait? What's this? My snowplow bill! Jumpin' Jehosaphats! My snowplow driver will be sending his kids to Harvard. I have to get a fourth job to pay my snowplow bill and afford to hire someone to shovel my roof.

You know what really chaps my hide? Why can't the plow guys and graders coordinate their schedules? Huh? As soon as my driveway is plowed, the grader comes by and makes a berm. Then I have to go out and shovel, shovel, shovel. It's a conspiracy I tell you!

Why can't those stupid snowflakes fall through the cracks of my deck? They are skinny enough. Why can't someone invent a heated deck? And a heated roof? And heated socks and heated clothes. How about a vibrating roof? That's it! I will invent a vibrating roof that shakes the roof and all those pesky little snowflakes will topple right down.

If one more spring catalog arrives in the mail I will personally rip the cluster box out of the ground. I tell you what I'm going to order. I'm going to order a blowtorch to blast the icicles and ice dams from my roof.

Today I have sunk to a new level and made a snow shooter. Kind of like a peashooter but more industrial, As soon as my neighbor goes to work, thwack, I am going to shoot my snow into his yard. Tee-hee!

February 2008
Hibernation

A rabid little groundhog predicted six more weeks of winter. Where? In Papagoochi? From my vantage point, the igloo on top of my roof, there's at least three months to go. Beware the person who says, "We need the moisture." I'll claim temporary insanity. I'm telling you we need the sun!

I am going back to bed.

Wake me up when the sun comes out. ·

I've Got the Genes for Embarrassing Moments

There are two kinds of people in this world. Those who can wear a white shirt and eat spaghetti with marinara sauce and those who wear marinara sauce on their white shirt when eating spaghetti.

I think it has something to do with chromosomes. Either you get a gene labeled "Embarrassing Moments" or you don't. I know I have such a gene because embarrassing moments happen to me with alarming regularity.

I have had so many embarrassing moments while wearing ski clothes that you will never, ever see me skiing underneath a lift. I've tried to forget about the dozens of crossed ski tips and spectacular crashes but there is one incident that registered 9.9 on the Richter scale of memory. It happened a dozen years ago when I skied with Warren Miller. I was certainly not going to audition for a part in the movie. I am your basic advanced intermediate skier—good on high-speed cruisers and lousy in the bumps. At the time, I worked in the marketing department for the Steamboat ski area and I was assigned to make sure Miller and the folks he was skiing with had a good time.

On the last run of the day and I finally had a chance to ride the chair lift with Miller. I panicked. What would I say to this legend with the build of Schwarzenegger and the eyes of Paul Newman? Worrying instead of watching the approaching chair I barely heard the lift operator yell, "You're going to get hit." I looked over my shoulder and realized he was right. The swinging chair struck my left leg and down I went.

I can tell you Miller skis on very long, very black K2 skis because my face landed right on them. I stared at those skis a long time before I had the courage to lift my head. I tried to stand; lost my balance and fell again. The laughter from people in the lift line was deafening. "Put her in a Warren Miller movie," someone shrieked from the back of the lift line." That suggestion made the liftie light up like a pinball machine. He eyed Miller. "Are you Warren Miller?" he whispered reverently. Miller nodded. "Oh my God," cried the lift operator. "Warren Miller is riding my lift. I'm so glad she fell."

No one offered to help me up, as they were all too busy gawking at Miller. I no longer had to worry about what we would discuss on the lift as I spent the entire time apologizing while he gallantly insisted it was all his fault.

I sat next to Miller that night at dinner and watched the bus boys in the restaurant jockey for the chance to clear his plate. One bold one asked for his autograph and he signed a menu for another person at our table. I was grateful that all eyes were on him and not me as I stumbled on my way back from the salad bar. I kicked the cherry tomatoes under a chair and gave thanks that I wasn't down there with them.

I used to be embarrassed by my embarrassing moments. But recently I remembered a phrase that has helped me put it all in perspective. Once I heard someone say, "Angels can fly because they take life lightly." It made me realize that embarrassing moments are really a gift. They make us laugh at ourselves; they force us to lighten up and take life less seriously.

I've decided I want to fly with the best of them. And who knows— the next time I discover lipstick on my teeth, I may sprout wings.

Resist Temptation

Note: Since Dr. Phil never addresses issues confronting couples on the ski slopes I am devoting this column to skiing with your mate. The term, 'mate' applies to your spouse, significant other or the person whose clothes you frequently find on the floor. Out-of-town houseguests fit into this category as well. In this scenario, the male is the superior skier but the reverse, particularly among locals, can be true too.

It happens every ski season. Even if I were to ski only one day of the year I can practically guarantee that I will come across a couple stopped dead in the middle of the slope arguing with each other. In between the screaming and crying the following words can be overheard:

Woman:	"I told you, I couldn't ski moguls!"
Man:	"Just point 'em downhill! Let the skis do all the work."
Woman:	"Why did you take me on this run?"
Man:	"Let's play *Follow the Leader*. Turn where I turn!"
Woman:	"I hate you!"
Man:	"Ski over the tops of the bumps."
Woman:	"I hate you!" (She advances on her mate shaking a ski pole.)
Man:	"You're making it harder than it is."
Woman:	"I hate you! I'm going home! I never want to see you again!"

To avoid this argument, maintain a harmonious relationship and avoid sleeping alone on an uncomfortable couch, I offer this tried and true method for skiing with your mate.

Don't.

I repeat.

Don't.

Do not give into temptation. Do not try to be a good sport. Do not let him talk you into it. Just wait. Calmly but firmly state you would love to ski with him and be a part of his day *after* 11:00 a.m. Turn him loose to ski with his friends. Let him press glass, huff and puff to find some little powder cache or ski through the trees. Allow him the freedom to make two turns at Mach 5 speed on a freshly groomed run. Let him catch big air off a mogul or huck it off a cliff. At 10:50 a.m. your mate, tired and sore has a convenient excuse for his buddies. He just says, "I have to meet my mate!" He saves face because he doesn't have to admit he's exhausted, his quads are cramping and his feet hurt. You have become his savior and he will worship the ground you walk on and the air you breathe.

While he is busy busting out all the moves from the last Warren Miller movie, you have time to roll over and snuggle underneath the down comforter. Or pop a chick flick into your DVD player. Or both. Since no one is complaining and telling you to hurry up you have all the time you need to get ready. Into your ski outfit should go: a precious comb to combat hat hair. Lip stuff. A dab of cash. A stash of hand warmers. A cell phone.

There!

Finally, please pick an indoor meeting place, preferably with a bar for your rendezvous. There is nothing worse than shivering outside if he gets delayed. And if he loses a ski or drops a pole from the chair lift you can simply order another hot chocolate with a generous dollop of whipped cream and eavesdrop on a family from Chicago.

When he arrives, he will be so happy to see you. After two or three runs together it will be time for lunch. He will be grateful for the break and grateful to you for providing it. There is no complaining because by now you are a ski goddess to whom he must pay homage. He will buy lunch. He will carry your poles. He will wait patiently while you adjust your bindings. Life is as it should be and you can get ready for the best part of any ski day:

Après ski.

Chapter Eight: Life with Technology

In Love with Mr. Mail

He was everything I wanted. From the moment we met, I was smitten. As soon as my fingertips brushed against him I was head over heels. He wasn't handsome and he certainly wasn't rich. But he had other qualities. He was a communicator. We were simpatico from the start. Talking was effortless, it went on for days. He wanted to know everything about me: where I was born, my mother's maiden name, where I went to school—everything! We held nothing back. There were no secrets. What a listener he was! Sleepless nights, he was there. Bad day at work, he was there. Just listening. Never judging. Never interrupting.

Every cliché was our cliché. Every song; our song. Every sunrise, rainbow, moonbeam was ours, all ours.

Like most couples, we had pet names for each other. 'Honey' or 'Scoober' were not our style. I cannot write what we called each other.....they were too special to reveal in print. To add to the intrigue, he took it one step further and insisted on a password. Whenever we spoke he asked for our password. I thought it was sweet. Touching, even.

He had friends, lots of them. They spoke a secret language, 'Http' something-or-other. I never understood or could learn it but it didn't bother me. We had our own language. Yes, the language of love.

He thrilled to my touch. All I had to do to turn him on was touch him and he would begin to hum. Thoughts of him took over completely. His initials, E.M. were on my mind, all day, every day.

I thought I'd been in love before. I'd suffered through relationships with cads, cowards and commitment-phobes but when E.M. came along I realized it had all been a trifle, a passing fancy. Nothing more. Thoughts of E.M. consumed me. He was my first thought in the morning; my last at night.

I was completely and totally lovesick. I spent all my time with him. I drew hearts with our initials inside. E.M and J.P. I imagined a future for myself as Mrs. Mail.

And then, the unthinkable happened.

He disappeared.

Vanished.

Not even a good-bye. A farewell kiss.

There was no contact. I railed at the gods who would take my beloved away from me. I couldn't eat or sleep. I tried again and again to connect with him to no avail. I did everything. I lit a candle. I considered a sacrifice. I cried out our secret love password.

At last, when I could think of nothing else:

I called my Internet Service Provider.

"I'm lost without him," I wailed. "I can't go on. He knows everything about me. He holds all my history, my secrets."

They asked all sorts of questions: Had there been contact with a stranger? Something foreign?

And then they delivered the bad news. Not in person, but over the phone:

A virus.

"Is it deadly?" "Contagious?" I whispered.

They spoke about my beloved, as *if* he was an inanimate object, a mere machine. They suggested running an anti-virus program…into something called his *system*.

More questions: Did I have a back-up? A Zip drive?

Of course not! Didn't they get it? What we shared was personal, *intimate*.

What was to become of us? Did I have to start over with some phony baloney whiz-bang replacement?

An iPhone?

BlackBerry?

Not me. I am loyal. True blue.

I bought the anti-virus. I coaxed my true love back to health.

We were reunited.

We were one.

Not Just For Talking

Press one if you'd like to read this column in English. Press two if you'd like to bypass this column and go straight to your horoscope. Press three if you'd like to buy this column by waving your cell phone over it.

Cha-Ching.

Just when I thought I was the master of my cell phone, and not a slave to it, a new technological breakthrough may allow for something called "mobile payment." One smarty-pants credit card company is trying to turn the cell phone into a substitute for credit cards, allowing you to buy items simply by waving your phone at an electronic reader. It's a marriage of convenience. A credit-phone, debit-phone. This is like being the person in the back row of an auction house who, oops! buys something by scratching his nose.

Imagine being in the "you-scan-your-own-groceries-because-we-can't-hire-enough-employees-line." In front of you, the self-scanner customer is yelling into his phone:

"I couldn't find the rutabagas," says the angry person with wildly gesticulating arms. "You always send me to the store. You try to find the rutabagas next time. What kind of recipe calls for rutabagas anyway? $2,642! I just spend $2,642 at the grocery store? How did that happen?"

While marketers may think adding a credit card feature to a phone will simplify my life, it will only complicate matters. Do you know how many times a day I lose my phone and have to use another phone to call it, only to discover it's underneath a piece of paper on the kitchen counter? What if I really and truly lost it? Someone might buy a time-share in Maui and charter a plane to get to it.

Carrying a credit card does not inconvenience me. The .000001-ounce it adds to my load burns additional calories. Truth be told, I like the option of leaving it at home so I'm not tempted to use it.

Phone features have already gone far enough. I don't want to text message, play games or take pictures. My phone has a dizzying array of features that only a ten-year old can understand. A year ago I got it and it only took me six months to figure out how to save phone numbers in Contacts and I really felt superior when, on a trip, I figured out how to use the alarm clock. Most of the features I don't understand and I don't like the bossy manner in which they are offered: "Get Tunes & Tones! Get Pix & Flix! Get Fun & Games! Manage Music! Sync Music! Do this! Do that!

If they really want to enhance the cell phone here are some additional uses and features I would like to see added.

- Long board—If you run out of gas, your cell phone, at the push of a button, extends into a long board so you can ride to the closest gas station.
- Doorstop.
- Boomerang.
- Castanets.
- Evian phone—holds eight ounces of water.
- Hinge.
- Sunshade for your nose.
- Game piece for Monopoly.
- Bookmark or an itty-bitty book light.
- Hair barrette.
- Money clip.
- Add sand to it, close it and pull out a pearl.
- Salad tongs.
- Clothes pin.
- If you have two phones, use them as earmuffs.

And finally press four if you'd like to simplify your life and go back to a rotary phone.

This Time I Mean It

I am a liar.

This is a hard thing to admit, especially in print, because up until recently I've considered myself a scrupulously honest person. I have never lied about my age, weight, income or marital status. I might fudge a bit on my hair color but only because I've been highlighting it for so long I have no idea what the actual color is. I guess I'm a questionable blonde. However, a recent event made me realize I lie to myself on a daily basis. The big whooper, the five-word falsehood is:

I'll never do that again!

Here's what happened.

I am the questionable blonde owner of, Miss Pink, a Motorola Razor cell phone. I love this phone. The phone is everything I am not: slim, sexy and sleek. I use it on a daily basis for my personal and professional life. I tell time with it. I have whispered thousands, okay, bazillions of words into her ear. My phone has heard me cry, complain and croon and still she remains loyally in the pocket of my purse. I, likewise, am loyal and do not trade her in for another phone with more razzle-dazzle features I can't understand.

One day I looked at Miss Pink and her display read, "!!##??" I rushed my dear phone, my best friend, my confidante into the nearest phone hospital and they dispassionately pronounced her DOA.

Dead!

Furthermore they insulted the dearly departed by saying, "We've had more problems with this phone than any other."

And so, naturally, I placed an order for Miss Pink II.

A long, quiet 48-hrs. passed and then due to weather another 24-hrs. dragged by. I'd like to write that during this time I behaved nobly and enjoyed the peace and quiet. I'd like to write that I read Proust and engaged in a stirring intellectual discourse on foreign policy with my friends and family. But, no. I behaved rather poorly. I sulked. I whined about the weather. A lot. I battled my 10-year-old son for his phone only to be told, "I'll rent it to you for $5.00 a day."

That is when I heard the annoying voice, a voice I later recognized to be a liar start:

I'll never do that again!

I'll never do that again!

I'll never do that again!

I vowed when my new pink beauty arrived I would do everything to keep her dry. I would buy a waterproof case for Miss Pink II and not talk on the phone while around snow or other wet surfaces.

I was full of good intentions. I really was. But I am also busy. And so, two weeks after receiving Miss Pink II, I watched her slip from my grasp and sink to the bottom of a hot tub. I considered performing mouth-to-phone resuscitation but decided, even for a questionable blonde such as myself, that didn't make a whole lot of sense. I rejected other emergency measures: burying her in a bowl of rice (rice absorbs moisture) and subjecting her to the force of a hair dryer but in the end I simply called the 800-number for the insurance company on my son's phone.

And so I'm moping and sulking and not reading Proust around my very quiet house waiting for another replacement phone.

I'll never do that again!

This time, I mean it!

And the blonde part is no longer so questionable.

Press 3 to Send Me to Fiji

Ijust had the worst fight of my life. Not with a family member, co-worker or a stranger. Oh no. That would have been easy. Instead I pitted myself against an automated phone answering system. I yelled at a robotic voice. Railed against technology. Went toe-to-toe with option number two. The annoying voice asked me what seemed to be the problem and I snapped, "You are the problem. You are driving me crazy!"

False friendliness has always annoyed me. But when it comes from a computerized voice it's even worse. The relentlessly chirpy voice replied, "I'm sorry, I don't understand that. Let's start over." "Well understand this," I yelled and slammed the phone down. The thrill of victory lasted all of ten seconds until I realized, with horror, I'd have to start all over again. Arrgh!

Automation   1
Home Team   0

Not one to give up easily, I redialed. Naively I thought I knew exactly how to win this battle. I bypassed all the voice prompts by pressing zero—usually a sure bet to get to an actual person.

Did I want to enter my 16-digit account number?

Zero.

Did I want to hear my estimated wait time?

Zero.

Did I want to give a call back number?

Zero.

Zero, zero, zero.

Just as my forefinger began to cramp I got an actual person. Victory! I pumped my fist in the air.

Automation   0
Home Team   1

The actual person listened to my super sized platter of complaints and requests and did nothing. Nothing. She passed the buck right back to automation by offering to transfer me to an 800 number. "Can't you help me," I begged. "I don't want to start over with another automated system." "I'll transfer you now" she said, "but if I lose you, write this number down." I spoke very, very slowly, enunciating my words as if I speaking a foreign language for the first time.

"Do you know how weird that sounds? You are the phone company. P-H-O-N-E C-O-M-P-A-N-Y. You should know how to transfer a call, right?"

The only response was a long sigh. And then, she disconnected me.

Human: 1

Home Team: 0

Right then and there I gave up. This was a perfect opportunity for AFOG (another frickin' opportunity for growth.) I lit some incense, and practiced a relaxing chant I learned from the Great Swami Origami. I will share this chant with you, dear reader, for the next time you are frustrated with automation:

"Om, ohblahdiohblahdah. Howdy, oh Great and Divine One. It's been awhile but it's me, the really nice, kind person who just last night gave the last bite of my key lime pie to my son. I believe in karma but just this once could you make an exception? I'd sure appreciate it if you transmit a tiny swarm of killer bees through the phone line into the office of the person who invented the automated phone answering system. Thanks, Divine One. Om,ohblahdiblahdiblah."

Waves of bliss crashed over me. My consciousness shot up into the cosmic stratosphere. I was at one with the world and no longer needed to rail against the forces of automation. Images of the lotus flower appeared before my eyes and I relaxed into the organic cotton cushions of my couch profoundly grateful for all of life's blessings.

Ahhhhh......

Press one if you'd like a private session with the Great Swami Origami. Press two if you'd like to go straight to the horoscopes. Press three if you liked this column and would like to send the columnist on an all-expense paid summer vacation to Fiji.

For Emergencies — Or Everything

I just got a new phone. By the time I figure out how to use it I'll be ready for my next upgrade. I've already misplaced my owner's manual. But that's okay. Truly. Because I still have two CDs to view and a 70 pg. manual of shortcuts to master.

It's easy to understand the appeal of cell phones. They promise a happy life. They don't promise you'll ever figure out how to make a phone call, but who cares? You'll be busy doing other things....all while insanely happy. The brochures, websites and commercials show happy young people, happily texting, happily watching TV on their tiny little screens, happily dancing to music, happily taking pictures or videos and emailing them to friends and family. Occasionally they are even shown *happily talking on the phone.* It's really the marketing feat of the century. Business students will be studying the cell phone phenomenon for years to come.

"Just for emergencies." This the reason most of us got cell phones in the first place. We were only going to keep it in the glove compartment of the car and use it to call for help if the car broke down. And then one day on a long boring drive we thought, oh what the heck, why not make a phone call? One phone call led to another and another, then another, and then you can't leave the house without it even when you're on a walk because who knows when an emergency situation might strike? Not only could you be wearing dirty underwear when the EMTs arrive, but you might not have your cell phone to call your sweetie pie to meet you at the emergency room.

Then you upgrade.

Then the phone starts to accompany you everywhere you go and I do mean everywhere. You hope and pray no one can hear you flush, but your mother always knows. "I can't believe you're calling me from the bathroom!"

Then you upgrade.

You convince yourself you won't need insurance because the phone is just for *emergencies.* After all, you hardly use it. And then something happens. Disaster strikes. You accidentally flush it down the toilet, drop it into the dog's water bowl, leave it on the soccer field or back over it in the driveway. Then and only then do you get hysterical. Your phone doesn't work and you have to wait at least 48 hrs. for a replacement. It's too quiet. There's nothing to do. While you wait, you join a support group. You admit you are powerless. Your phone controls you and not the other way around. You jump every time it beeps or buzzes.

Then you upgrade.

When your new phone arrives you spend hours studying the ring tones. It's fun to look at the names and figure out what they might sound like. Bike bell is easy but antelope? Dimples? Et voilà? Caffeine?

Your friends begin to worry because they never see you. They get text messages in the middle of the night but you are so busy learning about all the new features of your phone you have no time to socialize. You need to synch your phone with your computer, download music, master BrickBreaker and other games.

You upgrade your plan. You need complete coverage. You need the world at your fingerprint. You throw out your calendar. There's no need for paper, you have a handheld device that chirps a reminder to you whenever you have an appointment. Your alarm clock is next to go. Your phone can do that. Goodbye calculator and camera. Out goes the iPod, in goes the headset to your phone.

Then you upgrade.

Then you give up your landline.

Your addiction is complete.

Printed in the United States
154300LV00001B/35/P